Modern Essentials

Rozemarijn de Witte
Photography by Hotze Eisma

SOMA
san francisco

Modern Essentials

© 1996 Uitgeverij Spaarnestad / Hotze Eisma
English translation © 1997 by Conran Octopus Limited

For information, address: Bay Books & Tapes, Inc. /
555 De Haro Street, Suite 220 / San Francisco, CA 94107.

Publisher: James Connolly
Editorial Director: Pamela Byers
North American Art Director: Jeffrey O'Rourke
English Translator: Stephen Challacombe
North American Editors: Erika Sloan, Barbara Tannenbaum
Illustrator: Edith Buenen

SOMA Books is an imprint of Bay Books & Tapes, Inc.

Originally published 1996 by Uitgeverij Spaarnestad as
Persoonlijk Wonen. First English edition published 1997
by Conran Octopus Limited as *Contemporary Chic.* This
North American edition published 1997 by SOMA Books,
by arrangement with Conran Octopus.

SOMA Books may be purchased for educational, business, or
sales promotional use at attractive quantity discounts. Please
contact Bay Books & Tapes / 555 De Haro Street, Suite 220 /
San Francisco, CA 94107.

ISBN 1 57959 000 4

Library of Congress Cataloging-in-Publication Data: Witte,
Rozemarijn de. [Persoonlijk wonen. English] Modern essen-
tials / Rozemarijn de Witte ; photography by Hotze Eisma.
p. cm. Simultaneously published in London under title:
Contemporary chic. Includes index. ISBN 1-57959-000-4
(hardcover) 1. Interior decoration—United States—History
—20th century--Themes, motives. 2. Interior decoration
accessories—United States. I. Title. NK2004.W5813 1997
747.2' 13—dc21 97-30190 CIP

10 9 8 7 6 5 4 3 2 1

Distributed to the trade by Publishers Group West
Printed in China

Contents

Modern Essentials

CHAPTER 1

Natural

Creating a natural home

The natural look for the home is created by using colors drawn from nature, such as **sand, rich earth shades, white and a hint of yellow.** Of course, natural materials also belong in this decorative scheme: linen, fresh cotton, cane, wicker and wood. The great thing about using natural colors is that they allow plenty of freedom of choice in the **look and design** of your furniture, so that whether you choose country, modern or colonial-style pieces, the end result will always be **restful and warm.**

Natural

From simple to country style

1

CONTENTS

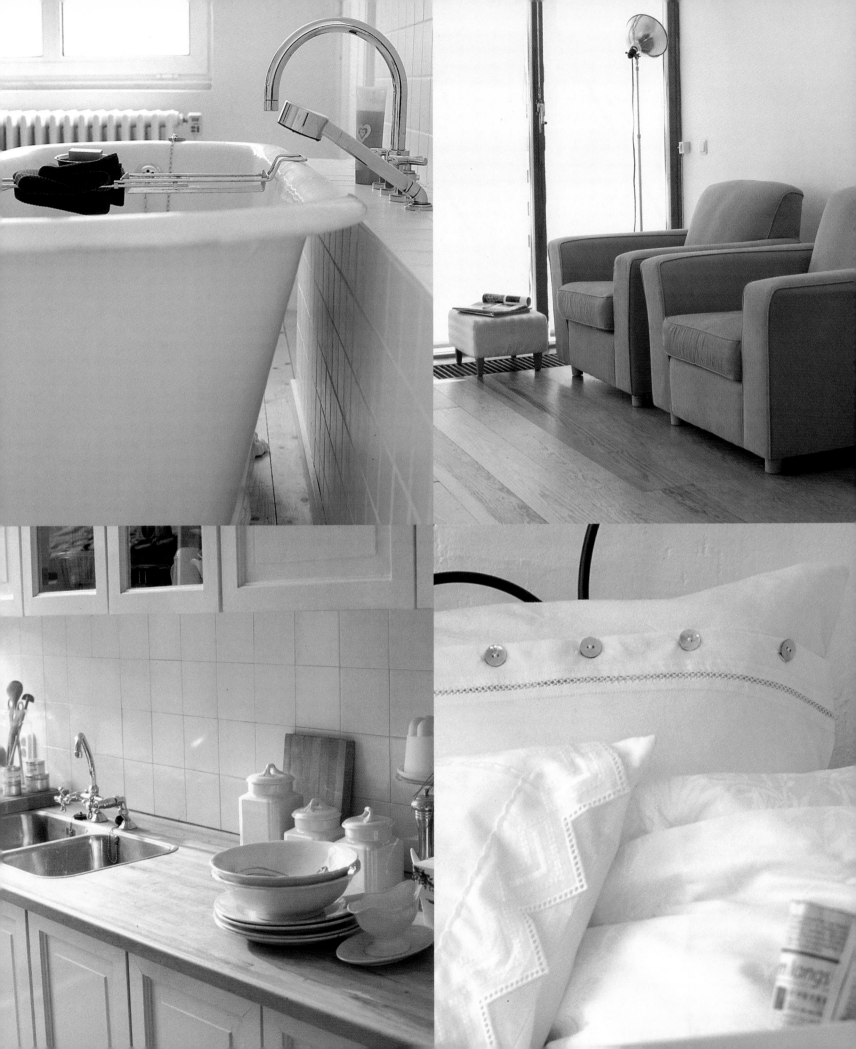

Natural

THE NATURAL
COLOR PALETTE

These colors are derived from natural objects in their purest form. The possibilities within this range are vast and the paint colors shown here represent a mere sample of those available. After all, which colors do *you* find natural? Is it creamy unbleached linen or golden barley rustling in the breeze? Is it unvarnished pine, rainwashed gray pebbles or a fox's tawny coat? Most important is combining your colors successfully.

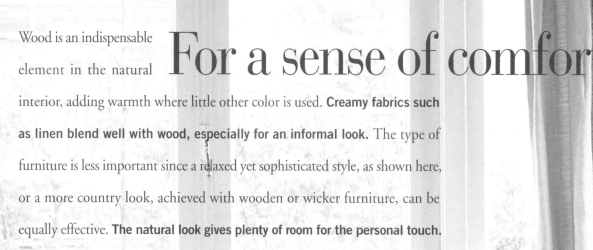

Wood is an indispensable element in the natural **For a sense of comfort** interior, adding warmth where little other color is used. **Creamy fabrics such as linen blend well with wood, especially for an informal look.** The type of furniture is less important since a relaxed yet sophisticated style, as shown here, or a more country look, achieved with wooden or wicker furniture, can be equally effective. **The natural look gives plenty of room for the personal touch.**

SPACIOUS LIVING

The natural home should have a sense of spaciousness. This is possible in a small home by using fewer but larger pieces of furniture – an immense gilded mirror, for example, to create an illusion of space, a large and inviting sofa, and curtains sweeping down to the floor.

MAKING YOUR OWN CURTAINS

These simple linen curtains complement the varnished wood floor and the bleached colors of the furniture. They are made by sewing two layers of fabric together: an outer layer of linen and a lining of unbleached cotton. The result is heavy curtains that create a feeling of luxury.

PAINTED CHIC

These pages show how varied the natural look can be: the country style on the one hand, compared with a restrained, modern look on the other. Here, the wooden fireplace mantel has been given a coat of gloss paint. The chimney in this type of 1930s house was usually designed for gas fires, and so a large open hearth will normally not draw well. To create a draft, a ventilator has been fitted to the top of the chimney and a glass plate positioned in the fireplace.

Right

A DIVIDING WALL OF WOOD

A plain wall of Douglas fir veneer separates the dining area from the kitchen and hallway. The table is of the same color wood, thus creating visual harmony. The natural sobriety is echoed in the row of bottles, each with a single, deep-pink tulip.

The natural styles

SHUTTERS AS SCREENS

Wooden window shutters can be used as screens or, as here, to add interest to a wall. They contribute to the feeling of spacious living, and the out-sized church candles are ideally suited to this theme. The marble fireplace, originally black, has been decorated with matte paint, to which sand has been added, to give the appearance of sandstone.

An eye-catching table

A room decorated to echo the mood of a country house, or an empty space except for a table and some chairs: these are the two extremes, **classical and modern.** The natural look blends seamlessly with both – and with every style in between. Unobtrusive colors and **simple designs** create a harmony of style.

Top left

NATURAL WITH GRAY

The natural look can be ultra-modern. By combining a concrete floor with a large blackboard and somewhat austere furnishings, an up-to-the-minute industrial look has been successfully created.

Top right

CLASSICAL

Pale chairs and white walls counterbalance an imposing cupboard of heavily grained wood. In this way, the classical look is kept light and airy.

Bottom left

A NEW WAY WITH LIGHTING

This table stands in the center of an empty ascetic space. To create interest, wooden chairs with curved backs and slatted seats have been chosen. The lighting solution is novel – instead of overhead lights, a metal standard with three directable spotlights is used.

Bottom right

A LIGHTER SHADE OF WOOD

The dark-colored wood of this table and chairs has been lightened with a transparent, white wood stain, then coated with a clear varnish. Better quality varnishes reduce discoloration of wood by sunlight.

Natural 17

Furnishing fabrics for the natural interior

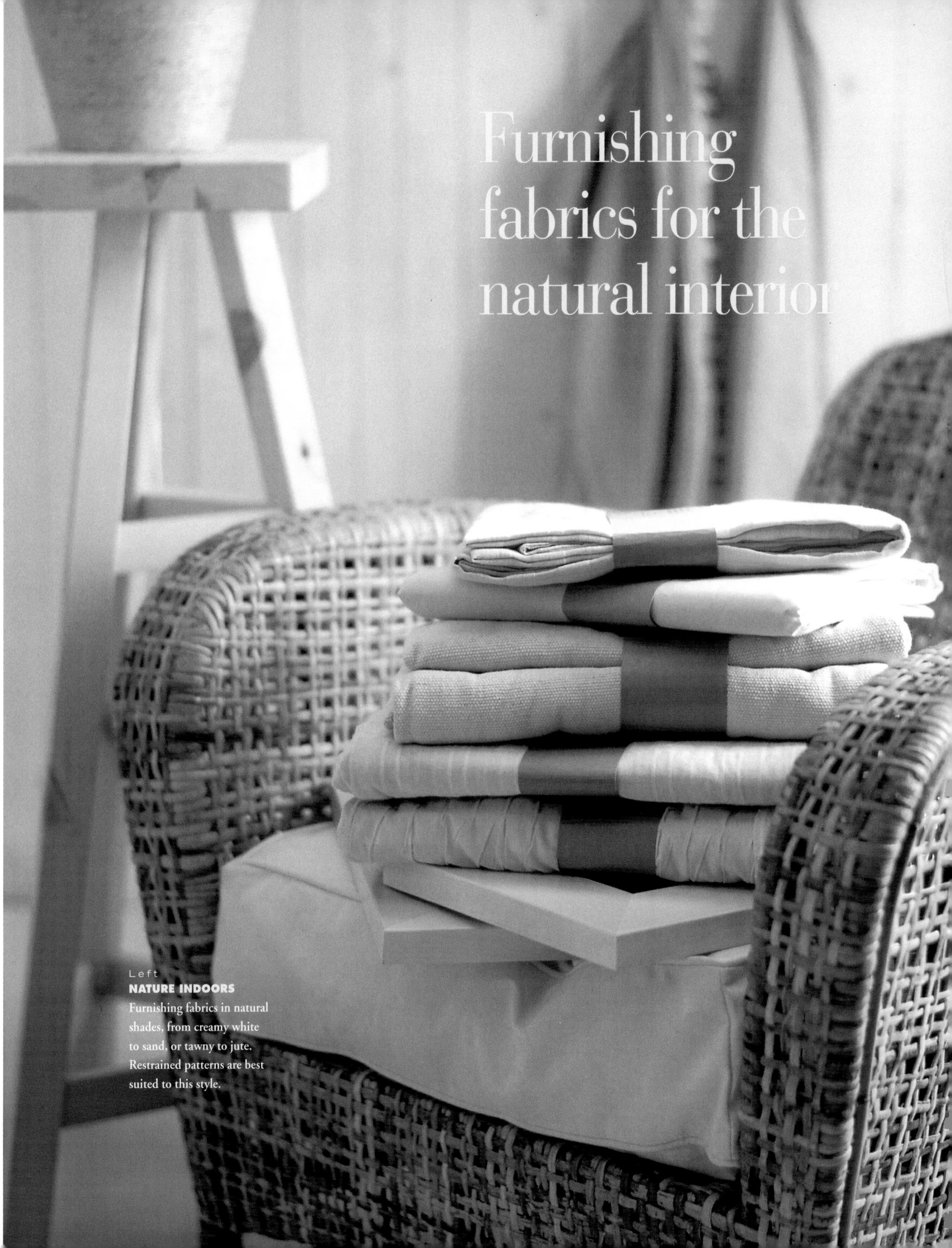

Left
NATURE INDOORS
Furnishing fabrics in natural shades, from creamy white to sand, or tawny to jute. Restrained patterns are best suited to this style.

Top and bottom left
OLD AND NEW TABLEWARE
Creamy white china goes well with natural-colored furnishings. Look out for odd pieces that you like at garage sales or flea markets. They will combine easily through color to form a complete service.

Center left
NEW BLADES FOR OLD
Old knives with bone handles usually have blades that have oxidized over the years. If the handle is too good to throw away, replace the blade with a new one of stainless steel. Seek them out in antique shops specializing in cutlery and silverware.

Right
OIL AND VINEGAR IN FINE BOTTLES
Part of living the good life is eating well, and that includes using virgin olive oils and spiced vinegars. Gourmet shops sell many different varieties of oil and vinegar.

Far right
SHOP COUNTER AS DRESSER
A long shop counter is used to display a collection of food covers, jars and other glassware, including cake stands. Large-scale counters and display cabinets can be obtained through antique dealers.

Living well

The country atmosphere is associated with warmth, sociability and a sense of security, where you feel at ease among furniture and possessions that have a story to tell. Many collections and **personal bits and pieces** help to create this atmosphere, whether they are made of glass, earthenware, wicker or wood. The greatest fun is to be had at yard sales and flea markets searching for that one missing item you have been after for years.

Top left
TWO-COLORED

Old stair treads are often so worn that it is a good idea to nail new ones on to them. By painting the stair treads a warm brown instead of white, greater depth is given to the staircase and a link is created with the floor of the landing.

Center left
MEZZANINE FLOOR

The different levels between bathroom and bedroom are linked by steps.

Bottom left
ROUND AND STRAIGHT

Every line of this staircase is rigidly straight except for the curved supports for the treads. The materials used – wood, metal and concrete – create an industrial looking hallway, which is also natural in style.

Right
MADE TO MEASURE

There was no staircase in this former coach house, so the family designed their own. The stairs are suspended over the stairwell and are made of hardwood treated with oil.

Far right
A DOOR ON THE STAIRS

To prevent all the warmth escaping to the attic, the owners of this home have sawn in half lengthwise an old door left over from remodeling work. Positioned on the fourth tread of the staircase, the door fits exactly into the small area of ceiling that partially extends over the stairs.

Custom-made, adapted to meet new requirements, painstakingly stripped: unpainted wooden staircases, in which **the wood grain is revealed,** contribute enormously to the overall country atmosphere. The natural, rustic look of untreated timber works particularly well with **white gloss-painted** doors and windows in the hall or on the landing.

A choice of stairs

NATURAL TREADS
Natural treads are best coated with a special floor varnish that is resistant to wear. If this makes them too slippery, cut grooves at the front of the tread to take small rubber, anti-slip strips, available from builders supply outlets. Where the steps are past renovation, new ones can be fitted.

THE COLOR OF A FRENCH FARMHOUSE

If you have yet to choose the colors for your bedroom, it is a good idea to base them on the colors in a painting you intend to hang there. What makes this wall so attractive is the way it has been sponged to resemble the external wall of a French farmhouse.

Left
ALTERNATIVE DECOR

This bedroom creates a feeling of modest luxury. The walls are painted off-white and the bed is not a focal point. An unusual chandelier of goose feathers and a glass display cabinet have been chosen to decorate the room instead of works of art on the wall.

Right
NEATLY IN RHYTHM

All the clothes are placed on identical hangers so that everything hangs at the same level, making them easy to find.

For modest luxury

Blue in the bedroom creates a **calm, restful and luxurious** atmosphere, and natural colors can have the same effect. A wall washed in beige, combined with bedding of cotton and linen, gives the bedroom **a country feel,** or, with the addition of broken white, a **more classical** style. The bedroom should be a place in which you can revive yourself.

Letting in the light

OPENING UP FOR MORE LIGHT

Built-in wardrobes between two bedrooms can be opened up (and the wall removed) if a bedroom suite is desired. Here, two casement doors have been placed in the wall so that the glass lets in plenty of light. The architrave was made by a millworks to match the existing mouldings in the house.

Top left

A CLASSICAL WROUGHT-IRON BED

This modern iron bedframe, decorated with romantic coils, is a variation on the antique bedstead. The little table is ideal for breakfast in bed.

Top right

SIMPLICITY IS BEAUTIFUL

Natural also means pure – a theme that is carried through in this bedroom by a minimum of decoration. Everything is kept simple, from the bedding to the doorknobs.

Bottom left

A BRIGHT ATTIC ROOM

An attic room can be made light and airy by painting the walls and roof white; this also helps to avoid the feeling that the roof is closing in on you. Insulation material is covered by painted planking.

Bottom right

OPEN FIREPLACE IN THE BEDROOM

There were at least four fireplaces in this house. What could be more romantic? The tall candlesticks lined up on the mantelpiece introduce an elegant touch to an otherwise cosy and informal room.

NATURAL FLOORS

In an unusual combination of hard and soft materials, a **LINOLEUM** border is inset into a **SISAL** floor-covering. **TILES** with an 'antique' glaze create the appearance of flagstones but are less porous. **RUSH MATTING** is an ancient material that once kept the floors of fishermen's homes warm and is now highly regarded for its roughly textured appearance.

OLD WOOD BLOCKS can be bought from architectural salvage yards. They look good laid in patterns. Solid parquet can also be used.

Simple **FLOOR TILES**, with a Mediterranean look, are also suitable for indoors. This bouclé carpet looks like sisal but, in fact, is made of **WOOL**, combining the soft texture of wool with the raw appeal of sisal.

Real **SISAL** can now be found in a wide range of colors, including many natural shades.

The color of **TERRAZZO** is determined by the color of the base concrete and that of the stone and glass fragments set into it. Here creamy white, light yellow and russet fragments have been used.

PINE FLOOR

This pine floor was stained the burnt orange color of Oregon pine, not just because the people who live here like it, but also to prevent discoloration by the sun. The floor was then varnished for protection.

WOOD COLOR TO TASTE

Certain woods are no longer available commercially for environmental reasons, while others are prohibitively expensive. By applying wood stain to ordinary pine flooring purchased at the local builders supply store, a realistic imitation of reddish-brown mahogany or red cherry wood is created without spending a great deal of money.

The warmth of wood, the practicality of tiles, or the combination of both of these properties in linoleum. **Old materials or new**: with a natural interior and neutral furnishings, there are many variations to choose from when it comes to flooring.

Floors with warmth

With the character of the past

Far left
MODERN OAK
The people who live in this house designed their own kitchen in oak, and had a cabinetmaker fabricate it. The combination of oak furniture and a stone floor creates a country atmosphere.

Left
ORIGINAL CUPBOARD
An old storage cupboard can be given a facelift by the addition of new doors, in this case glazed ones.

Top right
TIDIED AWAY
There is plenty of space for groceries, tableware and pots and pans in this custom-made, oak kitchen cupboard.

Center right
NOSTALGIA: A STONEWARE SINK
This kitchen sink made of stone, with its tall faucet, is deep enough to take buckets for filling and plant pots for watering. The worktop should overlap the sink slightly to hold it securely in place.

Bottom right
RUSTIC CHARM
A solid wooden butcher's block makes a convenient and robust surface for preparing food.

Today's natural-style kitchen combines **the convenience of the present with a nostalgic love of the past.** Modern ingenuity hides behind panel cupboard doors, with beech countertops, a stoneware basin and an original storage cabinet fitted with new glazed doors. The traditional farm-style kitchen, in which the entire family would gather for the evening, **encourages sumptuous cooking and enjoying leisurely meals at home.**

Classic cream with beech

PLAIN WHITE TILING
Just like the white-tiled walls at the butcher's, these tiles are seamless; in other words, they are laid touching each other with no grout in between. This is simple to do, even for those less skilled at do-it-yourself work. The width of the cupboard doors varies. Only those hiding the washing machine and refrigerator were made to a prescribed size.

Top left
SHOWING OFF

The farmhouse look is created
by displaying the dinner service
on a dresser. In the past, only
the best porcelain was shown
off in this way, but even
simple, everyday china looks
special on open shelves.

Top right
OLD WOOD

Old wooden planks make
lovely kitchen cupboard doors
and create a country kitchen
look. They combine well with
the stone floor and worktop.
The handy rail in front of the
oven is ideal for drying dish
towels.

Bottom left
HARMONY WITH COLOR

The family who live in this
house wanted a link between
the kitchen and dining-room,
so they bought oak from
a lumber yard for both
the dining-room floor and the
kitchen cupboards.

Bottom right
COLLECTING A DINNER SERVICE

It is possible to collect antique
dinner services by keeping
an eye open at flea markets,
auctions, and antique and junk
shops. It is a good idea to
research the prices your chosen
service commands, so that you
can spot a real bargain.

Top left
NEW BANISTER

Although the right-hand banister of this staircase was in good repair, the left-hand side and the balusters were replaced by a carpenter, who matched the detailing of the original.

Center left
TWO INTO ONE

Two built-in cupboards next to each other could be made into one wider wardrobe by removing the wall between them and their shelves. The two old doors are set off by a generous baseboard.

Bottom left
OLD BEAMS

A new window has been installed in the roof of a former carriage house to let in more light. The original beams have been sanded and treated with wood stain.

Right
PANELLED DOORS FOR BUILT-IN WARDROBES

Five old doors close off a built-in wardrobe. The depth of the closet was determined by the size of the central heating unit installed inside. The walls are finished in the same way as the ceiling.

Far right
A LIGHT AND AIRY ATTIC

Where there was once a small window, a large dormer has been built with French doors. The doors were the starting point of the project and were purchased from an architectural salvage yard. The attic was insulated and then covered with tongue-and-groove planking rather than sheetrock.

Working in the attic

Those who work regularly **at home** may be able to create a study or workshop in the attic. Many attics are used for storage, but there's often a great deal of wasted space. With built-in cupboards, efficient insulation, a dormer window to let in light and an off-white paint for the wood, the attic can become both an excellent **study or workshop and storage area.**

ATTENTION TO DETAIL

With the natural look, it is the small details that determine whether or not you achieve the desired result. Items such as porcelain or metal doorknobs and door handles can be found at architectural salvage yards.

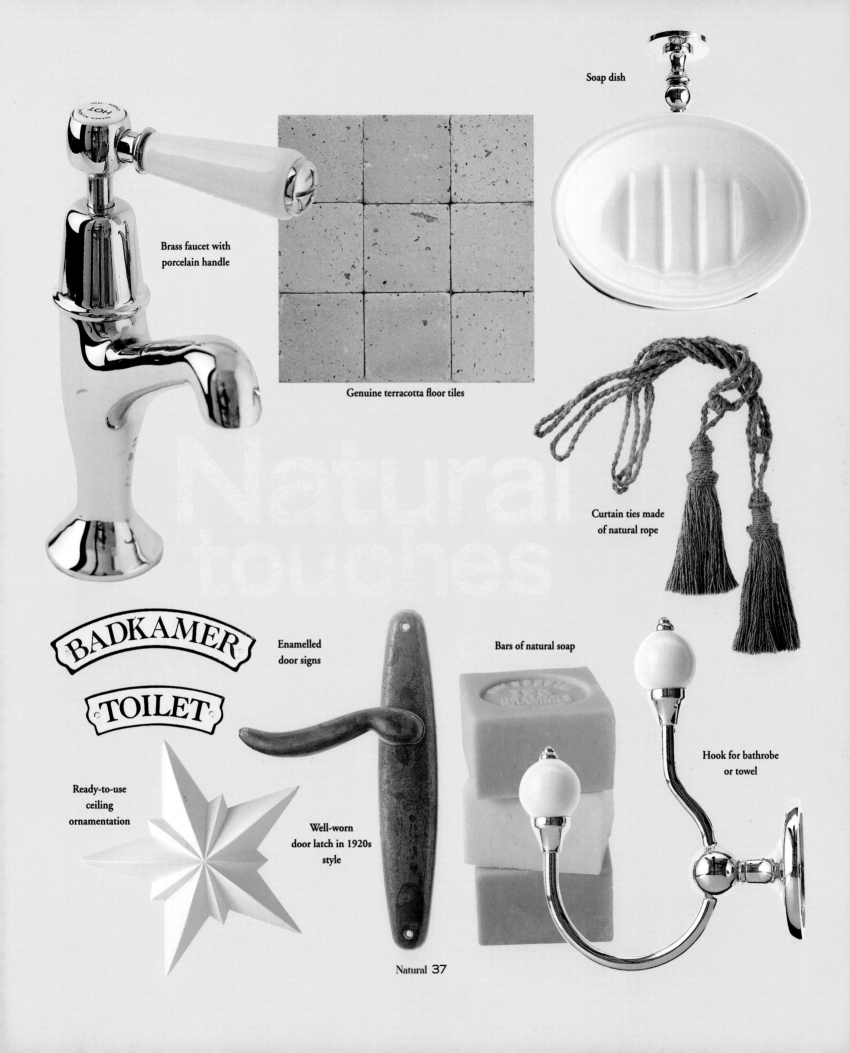

Brass faucet with
porcelain handle

Genuine terracotta floor tiles

Soap dish

Curtain ties made
of natural rope

Enamelled
door signs

BADKAMER

TOILET

Bars of natural soap

Hook for bathrobe
or towel

Ready-to-use
ceiling
ornamentation

Well-worn
door latch in 1920s
style

THE RIGHT PLACE
An old bathtub is best situated with plenty of room around it, although this does mean that the faucets will need to be connected to plumbing under the floor. An alternative is to place the bathtub against a wall, in which case the plumbing can be hidden behind panelling.

EXTERNAL BLIND

The louver blind is actually
fitted between two windows.
The inner window can easily
be opened without getting in
the way of the blind.

Far left center
NATURAL STONE

Stone does not have to be laid
in large rectangular pieces.
Used on curved surfaces, it
can be surprisingly seductive.
The soapstone and travertine
marble shown here have similar
natural patterning.

Far left bottom
IN STYLE

They look old but are brand
new. Various antique-style
sockets and light switches
can be found to match your
chosen style. Special safety
regulations apply to electrical
wiring for bathrooms.

Left
BATH ON LION'S FEET

A free-standing old bathtub on
lion's feet lends a touch of
times past. Ensure that the
wood floor is waterproofed by
sealing the joints and either
coating the wood with marine
varnish or coating it thoroughly
with preservative.

Right
PURE BEAUTY

It is the little details like this
delightful metal soap tray
hanging over the edge of the
bath that give a touch of luxury.

The natural-look bathroom calls out for simplicity, but just **how you interpret simplicity in your plans is entirely up to you.** The bathroom pictured on the left is unmistakably nostalgic, with the original enamel bathtub complete with lion's feet. By contrast, you can set your bathtub in a stone surround. Such a bathroom is also natural, but of **modern and uncluttered design.**

Old shapes, new ideas, pretty details

Left
SEPARATE YET TOGETHER
Two individual washbasins that are not inset make a small bathroom look bigger. The shelf above links them together and provides somewhere to put all the toiletries. Wood is fine in the bathroom, provided it is painted or varnished.

Bottom left
PRETTY AND PRACTICAL
No more will the soap slip into the basin. A liquid soap dispenser is also a practical addition to any bathroom.

Bottom right
A CLASSIC IN NEW CLOTHES
Pedestal washbasins are typical of bathrooms in older houses, and modern equivalents are widely available. The contrast between the old-fashioned basin and the modern faucets adds an element of humour.

Right
OUTWARD OPENING DOORS
There are many ways of creating the illusion of space in a small bathroom. Glazed doors that open outwards for a bathroom with little depth is just one of them.

The romantic style
of a seaside cottage

Soft Design

CHAPTER 2

Subtle contrasts soften a pared-down space

Basics are best is the simple philosophy behind the concept of soft design. It combines carefully thought-out design with a sensitive approach to color and texture, to give a room atmosphere and complement an architectural space. **Soft** is introduced to a room in colors, in curved shapes, and materials that positively invite a tactile response. **Soft** is emphasized through contrasts — matte against glossy, smooth against rough — a theme that can be carried through to the smallest details.

Soft colors, soft shapes

2 CONTENTS

Soft Design

**THE COLOR PALETTE
OF SOFT DESIGN**

These colors are pastel but not everyday pastel tints. The addition of a tiny trace of gray in most of the colors produces a more sophisticated effect, away from the 'baby' pastels of the nursery. Subtlety is the keyword – the soft green of a leaf after the first frost, or the delicate blush of a misty spring dawn. These hues go well with plastic and look good alongside matte metal or against bleached wood.

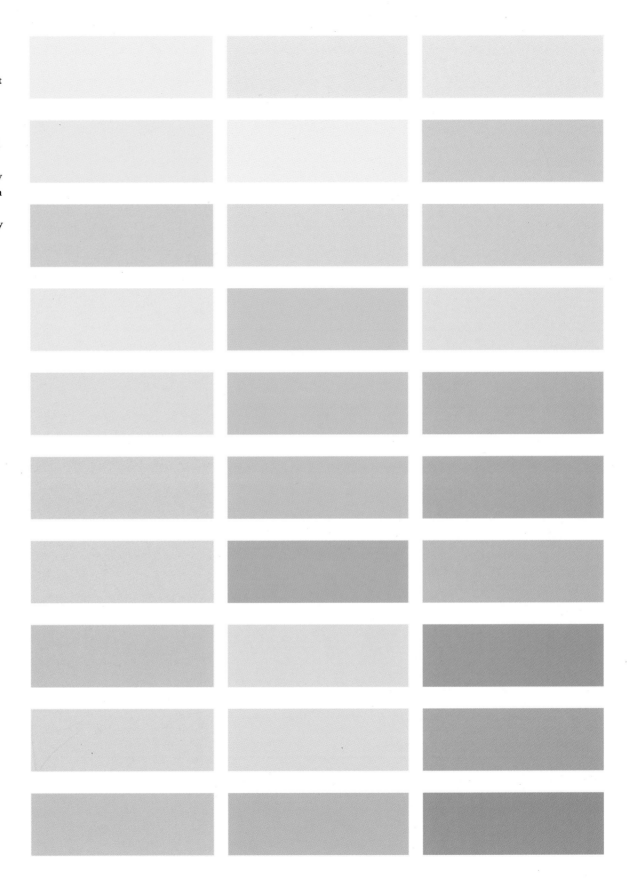

TRANSPARENT BUILDING BLOCKS

Instead of a large window in the outside wall of this home, a number of glass blocks have been set into the wall, each resembling a porthole to the outside world. These contribute to the room's tranquil air, together with the brightness and lightness of touch that is the hallmark of soft design. Gray tones contrast with the pretty pastel shades, and light fills the room with an ethereal touch.

Light, bright and spacious

Soft design is happily at home in a newly built house. **Lean lines are mixed with curved shapes** for a modern look that is full of surprises, yet still accessible and personal. This can also be achieved by using combinations of materials, such as steel and glass, plastic and concrete, mellowed by the **warmth of wood.** This spacious look leaves room for light to flood in.

**A NICE TOUCH:
TALLER BASEBOARDS**
The low baseboards that
are common in newly-
built homes can be
extended for an entirely
different effect. Adjust
the height of existing
baseboard by gluing
an additional wooden
moulding to them.

Subtle watercolors

Left

THE CLASSICAL WITH SOFT DESIGN

Classical elements work surprisingly well with this style. The light blue of the walls, the gleaming chest of drawers and the 'businesslike' gray sisal floor-covering provide an effective foil for the cream armchair.

Right

CONSIDERED SIMPLICITY

The L-shaped seating area is back in fashion. Everything in this room contributes to the feeling of spaciousness, from the large cushions to the real stone tiles. The design of the coffee table suggests that the inspiration for the room may have been Japanese in origin.

PLANNING THE LIGHTING

For furniture and pictures to be displayed to the best effect, the lighting must be in exactly the right place. The position of your lights should be carefully considered at the building (or remodeling) stage to avoid leaving any unsightly cables in view.

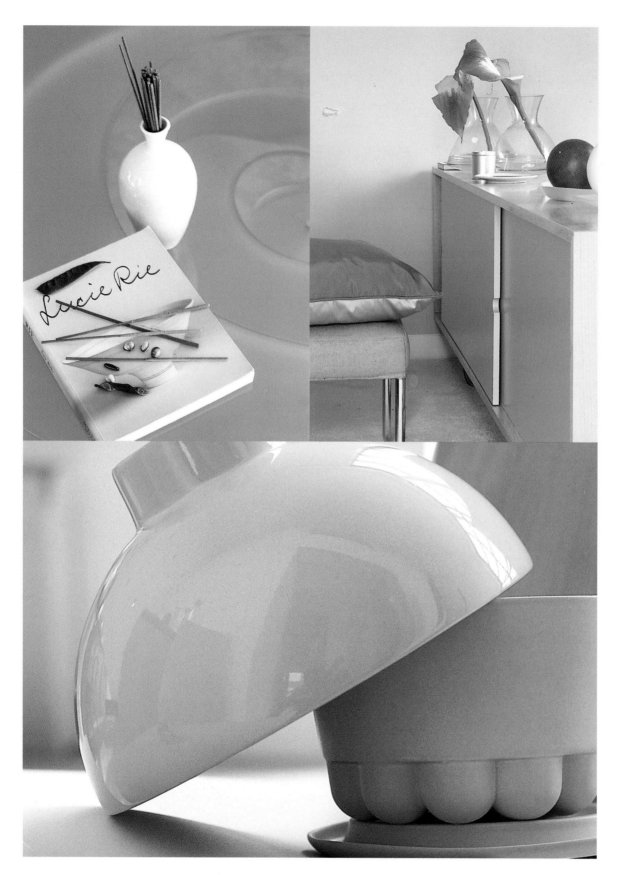

THE ART OF EXCLUSION

In some ways soft design mirrors Japanese aestheticism. It shares the subtle colors and the minimalist art of knowing what to leave out. But these rounded shapes give new life to the style, making it an interpretation rather than a copy of Eastern principles.

HARD MATERIALS, DELICATE COLORS

The cupboard and foot stool are sober and minimalist in design, but the delicate blend of pale blue, lilac and silvery gray colors creates an inviting feel, which is typical of soft design. An important element is repetition of form, shown here by the pair of glass vases containing identical leaves. This simple trick produces a strong, pleasing rhythm.

CONTRASTS: GLOSS WITH MATTE

Gleaming white china and matte earthenware in a subdued shade of orange act as foils for each other. This juxtaposition of items with different surfaces is a feature of soft design.

THE LOW DRESSER
Curved and rounded shapes, one of the hallmarks of soft design, contrast with the linear dresser on its long, slim legs. This is a reinterpretation of the style of the 1950s.

Subtleties of shade for modest luxury

Top left
JAPANESE WAYS WITH A BLIND

This translucent Japanese blind is a clever and convenient solution for covering a skylight. Held in line with the awkward angle of the ceiling by fixtures behind the rods, it is both practical and attractive.

Center left
NOSTALGIC SHUTTERS

Shutters are typical of French houses, traditionally made of wood or, more recently, metal. These streamlined accordion blinds take up very little space. To create a more Mediterranean feel, use wooden louvre doors, available from builders supply stores.

Bottom left
GLASS BLOCKS: IDEAL BUILDING MATERIAL

Glass blocks can be used on their own to pierce walls with light, or in rows to create a transparent wall, which also acts as a window.

Right
ARCHITECTURAL CORNERS

An opening in the wall which separates the living room from the landing ensures that the staircase is not completely shut off from the room. The steel banister was custom-made.

Considered details

Soft design includes small architectural details that have been carefully planned. These are **innovative solutions** that are simultaneously practical and pleasing to the eye, obvious yet unusual, and the traditional rules of design are thrown away in the constant search for them. **The strength of this style lies not in bold gestures but in lightness of touch.**

Top left
USING LIGHT

Steel reflects light while glass allows it to pass through. Plate glass separates the staircase from the landing, bathing it in light, and glass blocks introduce more light from a different source. A subtle interplay of colors is created by the many varying shades of gray.

Top right
FOCUS ON A DOOR

The porthole conjures up images of luxury liners from the 1930s. To solve the slightly awkward problem of a very wide doorway, the hinges have been mounted on the top and bottom of the door roughly two-thirds along its width. When it is open, the door then takes up no more room than a normal-sized door.

Bottom left
SYMMETRY AND COLOR

By glazing all the doors in this home, a continuity of style has been created. The doors are divided vertically into three equal sections, establishing a rhythm throughout the house.

Bottom right
ELEGANT SIMPLICITY

Soft green closet doors by Philippe Starck, extending from floor to ceiling, form a closet wall entirely in keeping with soft design. The simplicity of the design draws attention to the small detail of the door handles. The chairs, also designed by Starck, are simple self-assembly affairs of wood and plastic.

LESS IS MORE

This bedroom has everything it needs – no more, no less. The slim lines of the 1950s-style lamp and small table make them look almost weightless, an illusion that is echoed in the bed, which seems to float on air because the legs are recessed out of sight. The concrete floor underscores the simplicity.

RESTFUL, SIMPLE COLOR SCHEMES

For a restful bedroom, use the same color for the floor and the walls. Hold paint samples against the wall and on the floor to choose the color in the room's ambient light. Use the same samples to choose the floor covering.

Coziness without excess is the
secret here. Lavender blue is
well proven as a restful
color for the bedroom, and,
combined with butter yellow
and off-white, it creates a soft
mood which is accentuated
by the light filtering through
the translucent curtains. The
lamps, shelving and plain
bedding are kept as simple as
possible, and the squared-off
piles of pillows and bedding
provide a visual rhythm.

Tranquil simplicity

The bedroom can be **furnished minimally** in the soft design style. The only

apparent theme here is simplicity, but a delicate mood is created by the

choice and combination of elements, such as the slim lines of the table and

lamps and the plump forms of the pillows and bed. The coolness of soft

design makes a bedroom an **oasis of tranquillity**.

Fabrics to suit the soft design mood

SUBDUED TINTS
Unobtrusive shades, pastel watercolors and delicate designs are best suited to the rounded forms of soft design.

HARDWOOD THAT REFLECTS THE LIGHT
Light-colored woods are mainly used in soft design, but darker hardwoods are also appropriate if their appearance is softened with a light wood stain.

Businesslike with a lighter touch

Far left
A DESIGN EVERGREEN
The butterfly chair has stood
the test of time. The slender
legs (fitted with castors, if
required) and delicate shape
lend themselves to soft design.

Left
**WOOD IS HONEST
AND WARM**
Without the natural elements
of the wooden sideboard and
gourds, the stone and glass
table would create an entirely
different effect. Notice, too,
the restful color combination
of the warm-toned wood and
the lilac-gray table base with
its green plate glass top.

Top right
VERTICAL BOOKCASE
This simple, made-to-measure
ladder on wheels is practical
and also a work of art.

Bottom right
KITCHEN ISLAND UNIT
A modern solution to the
kitchen table, this island unit,
constructed from wood blocks,
has everything: double sink,
stovetop and drawers with
recessed handles. The wall
cabinets share the simple,
restrained lines of this style.

Now that increasing numbers of people work at home, the design of the

workspace is acquiring a **lighter touch**. Soft design strives for feather-light

answers that are both aesthetic and practical. Cupboards with plenty of

storage space replace filing cabinets, and industrial materials, such as metal

tubing, are **combined with wood** to provide the essential ingredient of warmth.

Finally, desk furniture is arranged to provide a pleasing visual rhythm.

Left
SHAPED TO FIT
The shape of the heated towel rack echoes the space, and the shiny chrome provides an eye-catching contrast with the tiles. Small mosaics are easier to work with than larger ones if the bathroom's design includes unusual or difficult shapes.

Right
SOFT DESIGN IS INNOVATIVE
Round shapes suit a bathroom well. They are pleasing to the eye, and the absence of sharp corners and angles makes the room that much easier to keep clean and safer to use.

UNDER-FLOOR HEATING SAVES SPACE
The chrome towel rack is intended to dry towels, so some other source of heating is also needed. Under-floor heating is comfortable and completely invisible.

Even when the rest of the house is furnished and decorated in a different style, soft design is perfect for the bathroom. **The combination of chrome and ceramics with glass mosaic** produces architectural details and gently curved

The bathroom

shapes that look as if they were specially intended for bathrooms. Small details can work very effectively in these circumstances. The result is a bathroom made for extended relaxation.

Top left
BARGAIN LUXURY

Luxury need not be expensive.
Face creams, bubble baths and
shampoos come in lovely pastel
colors and are often packaged
in attractive bottles. They are a
cheap way of adding a touch of
luxury to your bathroom.

Center left
THE STYLE OF
A SMART HOTEL

Attractive details work even
better in simple surroundings.
Take this into account when
working out your budget.
A small, quality item, like this
toothbrush mug and holder,
make you feel as if you are
staying in a first-class hotel,
and may give more pleasure
than expensive floor tiles.

Bottom left
PARTITION WALLS:
USEFUL AND ATTRACTIVE

Partition walls in the bathroom
can conceal plumbing and also
function as part of a shower stall
or enclosure. Here, a shower is
fitted over the bathtub.

Right
EXTRA LARGE
SHOWER-HEADS

Shower-heads are available in
many different sizes. Check
with a plumber that the water
pressure will be sufficient for
the type you prefer.

THE NATURAL COLOR OF MATERIALS

The glass door has a natural green tinge. Such subtle shades can be kept in mind when planning the color scheme for your bathroom. Thermostatic faucets are very useful because the water comes out at a predetermined temperature.

FINISHING TOUCH: EDGE PROFILES

Discolored moulding around bath and basin should be replaced with mildew-resistant products. Sharp corners formed by tiles set at right angles to each other can be rounded off with special metal edging. These can be tiled in the same way as ceramic strips, and the smoother finish on shower or bath looks much smarter

The power of simplicity

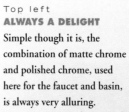

Top left
ALWAYS A DELIGHT
Simple though it is, the combination of matte chrome and polished chrome, used here for the faucet and basin, is always very alluring.

Top right
NEW LAMPS
The choice of suitable lighting has an amazing effect. A small, well-designed lamp highlights the other accessories.

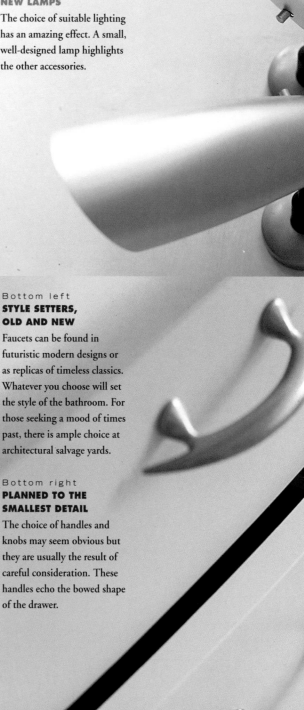

Bottom left
STYLE SETTERS, OLD AND NEW
Faucets can be found in futuristic modern designs or as replicas of timeless classics. Whatever you choose will set the style of the bathroom. For those seeking a mood of times past, there is ample choice at architectural salvage yards.

Bottom right
PLANNED TO THE SMALLEST DETAIL
The choice of handles and knobs may seem obvious but they are usually the result of careful consideration. These handles echo the bowed shape of the drawer.

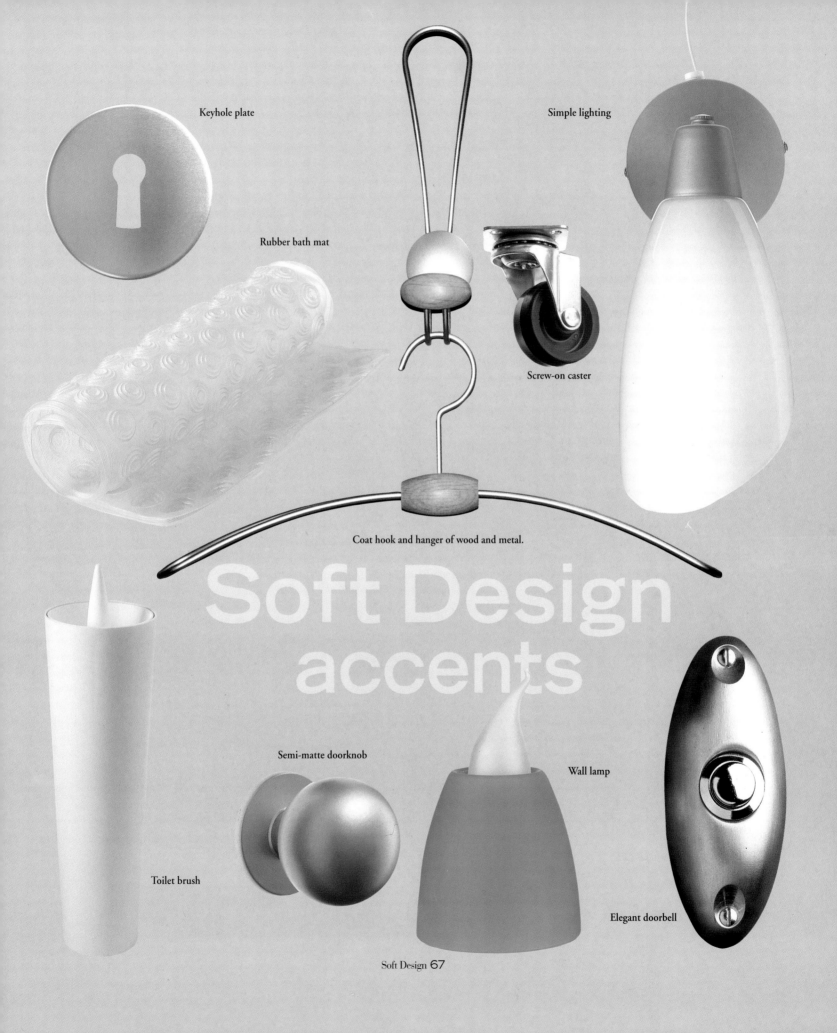

Keyhole plate

Simple lighting

Rubber bath mat

Screw-on caster

Coat hook and hanger of wood and metal.

Soft Design accents

Semi-matte doorknob

Wall lamp

Toilet brush

Elegant doorbell

Soft Design 67

Top left
BLOCK-FORM STAIRS

Stairs that are not open usually have treads that slightly over-shoot the risers. Although this might seem a small detail, the absence of such an overlap is very noticeable in this flight of stairs, which has the rather unusual appearance of blocks piled on top of one another.

Center left
STAIRS ON LEGS

This close-up of the picture below shows how the bottom of the stairway is supported just off the ground, so that it appears to float. The light and airy effect is increased by the way in which the metal tube disappears into the wood to reappear beneath.

Bottom left
SPATIAL DISCOVERY

This is an example of working within existing constraints: as there was only limited room for the staircase opening, it was given a curved shape. The stairs were constructed from wood similar to that of the floor, which was laid in a herring-bone pattern.

Right
SIMPLICITY IN STYLE

No extraneous detail is allowed in this staircase: there is just one support and cantilevered steps. The combination of black and white and metal is all that is needed to create the desired mood. On the landing, painted a serene white, there is the one detail: an unusual chair made out of cardboard.

TRICKS WITH STAIRS
Stairs that run between two walls are normally fixed at both sides. Here, a small gap has been left on one side, giving the impression of a very lightweight structure.

Architectural thinking

An architect once said that a house without stairs was a wasted opportunity. Indeed, **stairs can be breathtaking** and a wonderful addition to the spaces they join. Something wonderful can be achieved by **linking the design to the surroundings** and by selecting materials in keeping with the style of the house, whether the stairs are open or enclosed.

COMBINATION OF SHAPES

An optimum combination of stairs, banister and stairwell. The family that lives here had the banisters specially made by a firm that manufactures yacht masts and spars.

There are certain guidelines for floors in soft design: **light-colored woods** can be used to form **an attractive foil** to the more restrained elements of the style, and both sisal, **in tints of gray,** or carpet with a short pile, can be used to the same effect. Other options for flooring within this style are painted concrete, quarry tiles, mosaic and linoleum. Consider colors that mimic **gentle washes of watercolor,** such as silvery gray, sea green or very light blue.

Soft design floors

UNLIMITED DESIGN POTENTIAL

Glass and ceramic mosaic tiles lend themselves to fabulous designs in a huge range of colors. To strengthen the effect of the mosaic floor and to ensure that nothing detracts from it, the baseboard can be painted to match the wall.

CARPET with a very short, close pile, makes an ideal floor-covering for soft design. **LINOLEUM** is available in a range of colors and patterns. **TILES** look particularly good laid in rows. These are in slightly gray-tinged pastels, which resemble watercolors. **MOSAIC** suits any style. In soft design, shades with light color washes are preferred for the softer look they create. **KNOBBED RUBBER** flooring in gray creates an eye-catching, almost industrial look. **CARPET** in soft, pale colors combines well with metal and slender modern furniture. **LAMINATE** is available in many colors and designs, including the popular wood finishes, such as beech, which work well with soft design. **STONE FLOORS** complement soft forms and furnishings, and wooden cabinets. The choice available, from terrazzo to colored concrete, is huge.

DELINEATING WITH FLOOR PATTERNS

One space can be subdivided into separate function areas, for example, to indicate the sitting and dining areas of a dual-purpose room, by using different flooring materials or a change of pattern. A sense of partition can also be given by creating a border around the chosen space. Do this only when you are certain what furniture is to be situated where in the room.

Chairs naturally belong around a table but they need not be of the same design or material. In fact, it is a good idea to **choose chairs that are of a completely different material from the table** – glass, perhaps, with wood, or plastic with metal. You can also successfully **combine round forms with rectangular.** To finish, use a sleek lamp to direct light onto the table.

Around the table

PLAYING WITH CONTRASTS

These Philippe Starck chairs are made of thin plastic yet have the shape and bulk of upholstered chairs. The plate glass tabletop appears fragile compared with the massive base. The design is unadorned so that nothing detracts from its strong statement.

Top left
KITCHEN WITH A SITTING-ROOM FEEL

The kitchen has been installed in a low-ceilinged attic. On one side there is a sliding door and facing it the worktop, which is made from gray terrazzo without any added color. The aim was to achieve a sitting-room effect, with the worktop acting as a dresser.

Top right
NEW LOOK FOR THE 1950S

Scandinavian furniture designs from the 1950s are once again in vogue. Their best features are the slender legs and flowing lines with little embellishment. The table is made of plastic as opposed to wood, so that the attractive shapes of the chairs are not overshadowed.

Bottom left
INDOOR PATIO

The sense of relaxing on a patio with a cup of coffee and a sandwich or snack can be created indoors with a small table and some chairs. Add a book or newspaper, and the illusion is complete.

Bottom right
OPEN KITCHEN

The solid-looking wooden table forms a bridge between the kitchen and living room. As a range hood over the stovetop would have marred the lines of the kitchen design, a ventilation fan was fitted out of sight under the worktop.

MARBLE SURFACES
Marble can be 'tumbled' or 'polished': polishing produces a glossier effect while tumbling gives a denser surface which is easier to keep clean. Marble has to be cut to size with great accuracy, and a cardboard template is essential to show the exact placing of power outlets, for example.

Soft design in the kitchen is a **modern interior style** that takes into account your daily requirements, such as producing tasty and nourishing meals with quality ingredients in a minimum amount of time. These needs are taken care of with **practical kitchen design,** strategically placed appliances and easy-to-clean countertops. The style incorporates stainless steel surfaces, warm beechwood units, simple handles and useful racks, and demonstrates how **the functional and the aesthetic can be harmoniously combined.**

A new look at cooking

Far left
PRACTICAL AND AESTHETIC

The free-standing island unit is of double depth and has back-to-back cupboard space. Openings at the top of the doors replace handles.

Left
THE KITCHEN/LIVING-ROOM

Stainless steel, marble, and streamlined cupboard doors: there is something of the atmosphere of a professional restaurant about this kitchen. At the same time, the natural tiled floor, classic white tableware and rounded corners of the cabinet fronts clearly show that it is a room designed with the whole family in mind.

Above right
THE ALL-MARBLE KITCHEN

The entire back wall of the dresser unit consists of a large marble slab. Even the shelving, fixed in place from behind, is made of the same cool material.

Center right
A STYLISH SOLUTION

In a flexible kitchen layout, deciding where to hang dish towels can be something of a problem. Here, simple white dish towels are knotted to a rail: they look decorative as well as being close to hand.

Below right
THE RESTAURANT TOUCH

Well-designed kitchen utensils, containers, dispensers and dish towels are attractively arranged in a practical and accessible display. Plain white china or traditional designs would look equally good in this setting.

Top left
LIGHT HEARTED TOUCHES

Refrigerators and ovens influenced by American design of the 1960s are light-hearted introductions to the kitchen. The porthole in the oven door is a perfect soft design feature.

Center left
TRANSPARENT AND ROUNDED

Small details lend themselves to an entirely novel approach such as these transparent knobs.

Bottom left
FLOATING KITCHEN UNIT

This kitchen unit appears to float because its base has been placed far back out of sight. The drain-board finishes flush with the cabinet doors to provide neat, soft lines.

Right
GRAPHIC EFFECT

The division of cupboard doors and kitchen appliances creates an almost graphic pattern. Note where the door handles have been positioned, so that they form an attractive line alongside the oven.

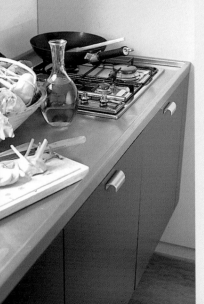

LET THE KITCHEN UNIT FLOAT

As shown on the left, a kitchen unit can appear to float in the air when its base is set back. This also allows you to stand closer to the unit, making it easier to reach across, which is particularly important if you have chosen a deep worktop.

Completely in style: 'soft' shapes

IN ITALIAN STYLE
Curved shapes juxtaposed
with formality is typical of
Italian design. In this kitchen,
the properties of the materials
used have been fully exploited,
as illustrated by the rounded
metal edge of the counter.

Handling details

Doorknobs and handles are more abundant in the kitchen than anywhere else in the home and they therefore deserve special attention. The type you choose will stamp its style on a cupboard door and contribute to the overall mood you wish to create. Whether classic or modern, formal or light hearted, suitable knobs and handles for the soft design look often include rounded features, which are **pleasing to touch** and work harmoniously with the overall design.

DOOR HANDLES MAKE THE KITCHEN An enormous range of handles and knobs for kitchen cabinets and drawers can be bought from individual suppliers as well as builders supply stores. These pictures illustrate just a few of the different designs and materials available.

CHAPTER 3

New Classical

A modern look at tradition

The classical approach to interior design for the home has always been about quality and form. The new classical style places this within a fresh framework. The color palette of **taupe, grayish-brown and the patina of worn silver** works beautifully with dark wood and subtle ornamentation, reminiscent of the colonial style. It is this combination of clean lines, simple shapes and neutral colors, lifted by decorative detail, that results in a sophisticated style with echoes of an elegant French home or New York apartment: **a timeless style rejuvenated.**

New Classical

Subtle colors and decorative details

3

CONTENTS

DE PSALMEN
Boudewijn Büch | Geestgrond

New Classical

THE NEW CLASSICAL COLOR PALETTE

Classical colors range from creamy white, through the natural colors of gray, brown and taupe, on to spicy ginger and cinnamon, finishing with the deepest midnight blue. Sophisticated and dramatic, these colors look superb with antique furniture, aged gold leaf and matte silvery metal.

New Classical

Divide the space differently

New times call for new ideas. How you decide to divide up the space in your home should be determined by your lifestyle rather than by tradition. Furnishings in the classical style have great potential because they have the same **strong presence** even when they are arranged in completely new ways.

When not in use, the dining
table and sofa butt up to each
other, and are placed centrally
in the room so as not to take
up circulation space. The dining
chairs are covered with Indian
cotton to blend with the sofa.

Top left
ROOM FOR DESIGN
The owners of this home painted the pine floor with antique stain and made ⅛ inch (3mm) grooves between the floorboards with a router. The custom-made cabinet behind the armchair has panels of perforated metal which conceal the music system, television and stationery files.

Top right
STATELY AND STYLISH
A fine entrance: the hallway links the kitchen and living-room. The chairs, upholstered in off-white canvas, provide an attractive focal point.

Below
MULTICULTURAL
These simple armchairs are upholstered in a suede-like fabric, which gives them a lived-in look. Traditional shields from New Guinea, in complementary shades of brown, provide an exotic touch.

Right
LIVING AROUND THE FIRE
An open hearth is the dominant feature in this room, and the seating has been loosely arranged around it. In such a setting, occasional tables – or in this case a lidded basket – are a better design solution than one central coffee table, resulting in far more open space.

Seating areas
with a difference

The finest furnishing fabrics

FABRICS FULL OF TRADITION
In the new classical style, warm-colored fabrics offset woods of different tones. Cream and golden shades against the sober colors of dark wood and pottery have a traditional feel.

Top left
FIREPROOF BRICKS
The brick fireplace was recently added to the front of a chimney consisting of twin-piped flues. Fireproof bricks were used to create a new fireback and surround.

Top right
MANTELPIECE OF SANDSTONE
The warm, rich tones of this sandstone mantelpiece are offset by the cool lavender blue walls and the golden hues of the wood floor, gilded mirror frame and armchair.

Below
ADDING SUNNY ORANGE TO THE PALETTE
The natural stone mantelpiece surrounding this fireplace is set against a wall painted in a warm earth color, which gives depth to the gray. Coarse woven mats suit the colonial look of the furnishings in shades of brown, sand and ivory. Two wooden armchairs have been placed on the other side of the coffee table instead of a second sofa. These are easier to move close to the fire on cold winter evenings.

Around the hearth

HOW TO USE A LARGE FIRE SURROUND
The size of a fireplace needs to be in proportion to the diameter of the chimney to ensure that the fire draws properly. Where the chimney is small, a large mantel can still be used if the opening to the fireplace is reduced, as shown here.

STAYING IN PROPORTION
The fireplace should determine the size and scale of furniture in a room, which needs to be in proportion to complement it. The opening to this fireplace has been reduced but it retains the symmetry of its mantel.

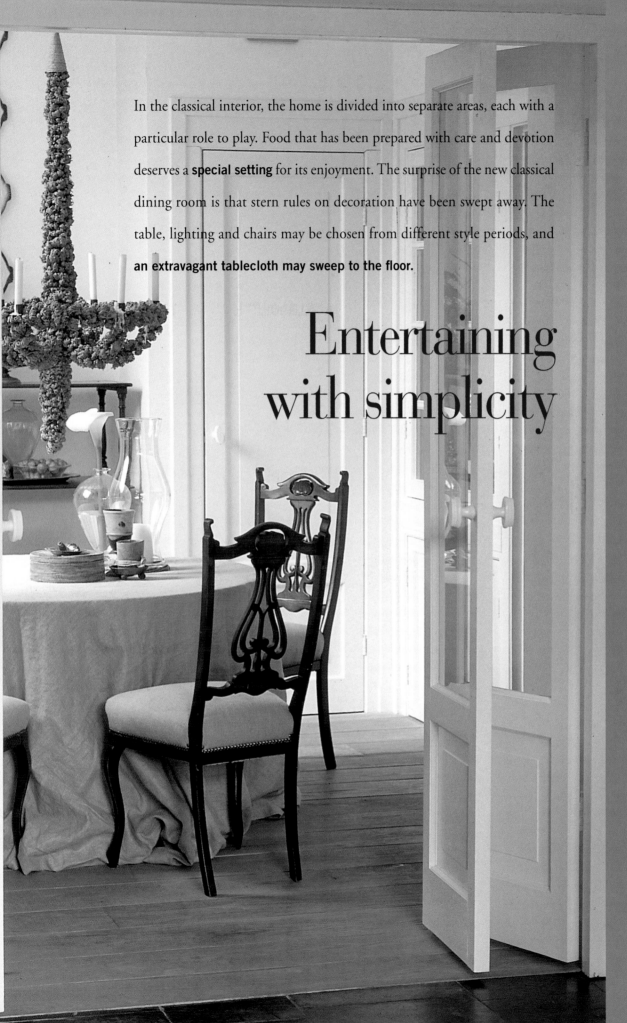

In the classical interior, the home is divided into separate areas, each with a particular role to play. Food that has been prepared with care and devotion deserves a **special setting** for its enjoyment. The surprise of the new classical dining room is that stern rules on decoration have been swept away. The table, lighting and chairs may be chosen from different style periods, and **an extravagant tablecloth may sweep to the floor.**

Entertaining with simplicity

Left
COMBINING STYLES
At first glance this dining area appears to be in the classical style, but closer examination reveals that it is a mixture of styles from different periods. The chairs are from the turn of the century, and the floor is of oak planking. The chandelier, a feature of the classical style, is given an up-to-date look.

Right
COLLECTING CHINA
This creamy white china has been collected from several discontinued lines to make an inexpensive dinner service.

Far right top
THE UTILITY LOOK SOFTENED
Modern design can be combined with the classical room. Plastic chairs are given a classical look by the addition of ready-made cream slipcovers.

Far right bottom
SERVING AS A SIDEBOARD
A corner of the dining area has been found for this small table, which acts as a sideboard, leaving everything within reach of the dining table. The white, antique dinner service is the perfect foil for the colorful still-life in its gilded frame.

A COLOR EXPERT
Since color is such an important factor in the decoration and furnishing of your home, it may be wise to seek the help of a professional color expert. These are usually people with artistic or architectural training who work closely with you to suggest color combinations that suit your own preferences and style.

FROM LINEN CHEST TO WINE STORAGE

Old furniture can sometimes be adapted for a new role. Here the lid of an old linen chest has been put to use as a door for a wine closet. The chalk on the string is used to write notes on the wines. The made-to-order table incorporates a useful slide-out section.

THEATRICAL EFFECT

The deep purple of the wall is an unusual but effective choice for a background against which to hang these gilt-framed pictures. Every evening, the candles are lit in the candle-holders mounted under the pictures; these were all found at flea markets and junk shops. The table is a masterpiece of craftsmanship and subtle design.

HARMONY BETWEEN PAINTINGS AND THEIR BACKGROUND

Art collectors and galleries used to base the background against which paintings were hung upon the tonality of the paintings. A wall filled with works of art in the home can be similarly treated. Little other decoration is required in such a room.

REPLICA DOOR FURNITURE

The handle and lock on this closet door are stylish replicas of an older design.

This niche in a closet is the perfect place for a washbasin. The oak panelling is protected from splashes by glass held in place with mirror screws.

CHROMED BRASS

Brackets such as this one, used here to support a banister, can be found in shops selling curtain rods and accessories.

BIRDS AS DECORATION

This detail from a door panel shows how attractive carved ornamentation can be. New architectural ornaments are available in a wide range of elements, from swags to single flowers, from which you can create your own design.

BACK AGAIN: WOODEN ORNAMENTATION

Plaster ornaments for ceilings have long been popular, while old door panels were often decorated with wooden designs. Now these are back in vogue, pressed out of wood pulp. They are also excellent for decorating mirror frames.

Made-to-order
picture frames

Chandelier drops

Gilded ornamental bracket

Curtain rods with
metal finials

Balustrade finial

Classical details

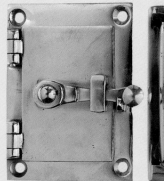

Door spy hole

Panels for built-in radiators

New Classical **99**

Top left
FOR SHOW

Highly polished wooden storage containers made from tropical hardwood gleam against the light background of a botanical painting. Objects displayed for pure enjoyment can look equally attractive whether grouped together or arranged singly.

Center left
RHYTHM ON THE WALL

Traditional art from Africa complements the new classical style. The intrinsic value of this collection is enhanced by the rhythmic way in which it is displayed, making it even more eye-catching.

Bottom left
BLACK AND WHITE

Snapshots, prints, engravings and old maps, all yellowing with age, tell their own story.

Right
SIMPLE IS BEST

Floral displays with an oriental feel are most beautiful when kept simple. This jar contains just two arum lily stems.

In the new classical style, **an exotic atmosphere** is created not only through decoration but also through the display of artifacts. Some pieces may be

From distant lands

unique objets d'art, others amusing memorabilia, such as candlesticks with 'leopard' markings, proving that distant lands are not so very far away.

Examples of classical taste are to be found at every point of the compass.

FRAMING-IN
Radiators can be framed in with a decorative wooden grille, so that they blend in with your chosen decor.

OUT OF SIGHT
Many practical items work well with the new classical style, but modern steel radiators are best kept hidden. Here warm oak was used to blend with the rich colors of the room and to form a deeper window sill.

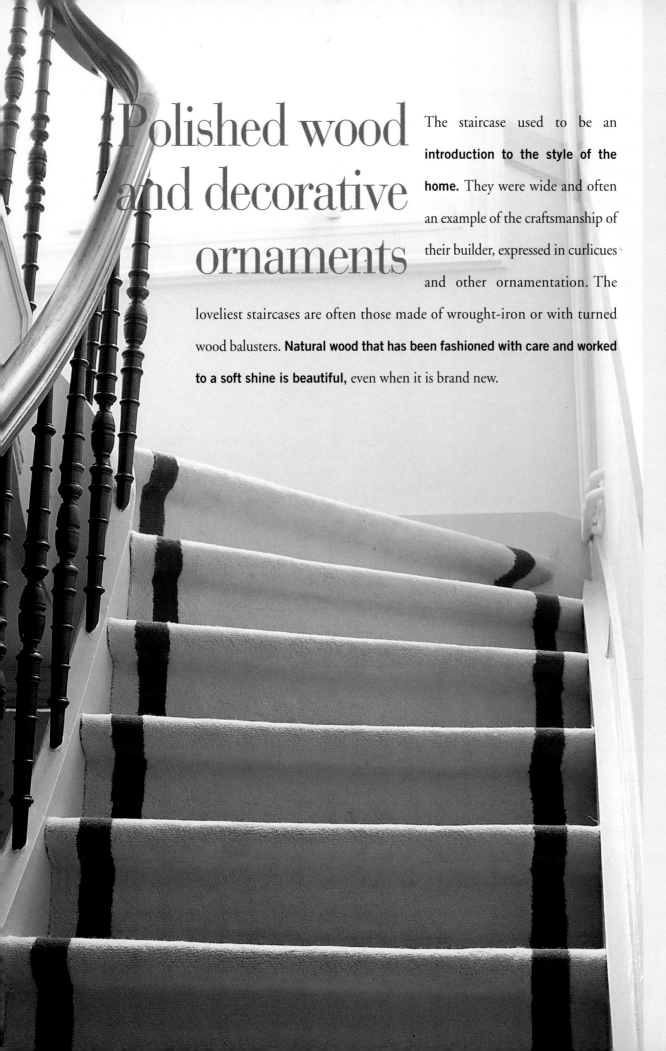

Polished wood and decorative ornaments

The staircase used to be an **introduction to the style of the home.** They were wide and often an example of the craftsmanship of their builder, expressed in curlicues and other ornamentation. The loveliest staircases are often those made of wrought-iron or with turned wood balusters. **Natural wood that has been fashioned with care and worked to a soft shine is beautiful,** even when it is brand new.

Left
HARMONY IN COLOR
The finely detailed balusters alone make this staircase attractive. If you live in an upstairs apartment, it is best to carpet the stairs, otherwise your neighbors will hear every single footstep. For a truly classical look, carpet only the treads.

Right
CLASSICAL BUT NEW
New stairs can be given an authentic classical look. High gloss varnished wood, with no ornamentation or embellishment other than its natural grain, plus wrought-iron banisters with a flourish of curlicues, provide a rich but contemporary look.

Far right top
STAIR RUNNER
A border has been cut out of this stair carpet and replaced with a contrasting strip to make the carpet look like a made-to-order runner.

Far right bottom
THE OLDER THE BETTER
The color of this oak staircase has deepened with the passing of time. The elegant balusters have an almost 'flattened' appearance, helping to create a light and airy stairway.

CONSTRUCTION OF SPECIAL STAIRCASES
Custom staircases can be made to suit your requirements by craftsmen or specialized fabricators.

WOOD IN THE BATHROOM

Boatbuilders know how to protect wood against water and to join it so that it is watertight. By closing any seams with rubber and treating the wood with heated oil, it is possible for wood to be used in damp places in the home.

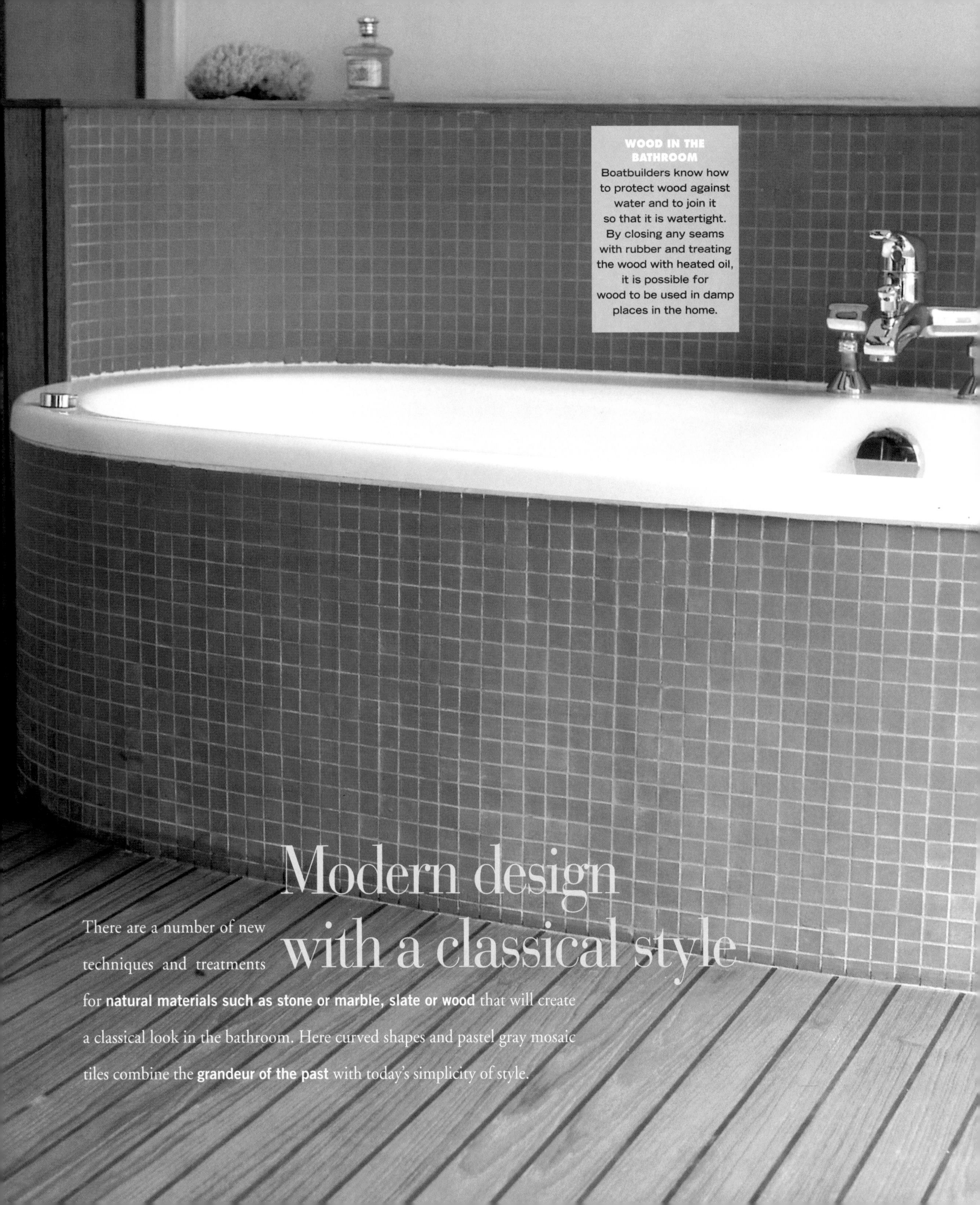

Modern design with a classical style

There are a number of new techniques and treatments for **natural materials such as stone or marble, slate or wood** that will create a classical look in the bathroom. Here curved shapes and pastel gray mosaic tiles combine the **grandeur of the past** with today's simplicity of style.

EXOTIC INFLUENCES
The blue and gold patterned
tiles in this bathroom evoke the
opulent palaces of the Moors.

**CLASSICAL MATERIALS,
MODERN DESIGN**
Although this bathroom
derives its classical ambience
from the use of traditional
materials, its modern design
ensures a fresh elegance. The
washbasin is set in a wafer-
thin black marble counter,
with a gently curving shape.

PLAIN AND SIMPLE
Plain wooden panelling has
been used in a small washroom
to enormous effect. This corner
is full of classical details: the
niche with its sink, mirror,
pendant lamp and glass shelf.

**THE CHARM OF
WELL-USED MATERIALS**
This ancient marble basin was
found piled with every sort
of object during a visit to an
architectural salvage yard.
As well as leaving the peeling
paint on the basin, no attempt
has been made to restore the
mirror. Signs of aging can be
charming, especially when the
objects are of good quality.

NEW MATERIALS

The rigid lines of stone can be imitated with a modern material such as Corian, which can be worked into any shape. This solid Corian washbasin is backed by a mirror of the same width.

PRESENT-DAY COMFORT

If the budget will allow it, why not invest in a spa bath with bubble jets? Your electrical system may require adaptation for this, and do not forget that there are strict regulations for electricity in bathrooms.

THE RIGHT FAUCETS

When choosing faucets you should consider the style of your washbasin or vanity unit. Make sure there is sufficient room behind the basin for the faucets to be turned on and off. Tall faucets require deep basins or the water is likely to splash onto the walls and floors.

TRUE SIMPLICITY

For this bathroom an unconventional approach has been taken with washbasins that give the appearance of two bowls sitting on a table. The simple wall-mounted faucets complement them perfectly.

Classical and modern in stylish sobriety

BETTER THAN STANDARD

There are standard shapes and sizes for everything in the bathroom, but perhaps a longer or deeper bath would suit you better. The same might be true of the shower. Instead of a standard shower tray you could have one made-to-order in non-slip tiles or terrazzo.

It is not just the furniture that determines the overall look of a room: the walls, curtains, ceiling and floor all play very important roles. With the classical interior, the floor can immediately set the tone of a room, even before a single chair has been put in place. Wood, brick and ceramic are natural and traditional choices that will lend an air of history and authority to any room.

A country house floor in your home

BROAD PLANKS FOR A PERIOD LOOK

The pine floor has been treated with antique wood stain and the gaps between the floorboards made intentionally wide to enhance the period effect. Pre-war styling has influenced the furniture design.

TERRACOTTA TILES give the air of a farmhouse kitchen but have the advantage in a bathroom of being non-slip.

SMALL MOSAIC TILES are versatile and can be laid in almost any pattern you choose. Their use in bathrooms dates back to Roman times.

PARQUET is floor-covering with a historical look. In order to achieve the country house style, lay a darker inset border.

STONE FLOORS can be given a shiny finish using oil but they look equally attractive when left with a matte finish.

QUARRY TILES decorated with colorful patterns are now widely available.

MOSAICS can be laid quickly and easily to fit any area. If the floor is not a true rectangle or square, the edges can be laid piece by piece. Ceramic mosaic tiles, which are less well known, look most attractive laid in an irregular pattern.

WOOD can also be used in wet areas, thanks to modern waterproofing treatments.

TERRAZZO can be broken up with borders of glass mosaic. The two materials are polished to form a smooth surface.

LOOKING AFTER NATURAL FLOORING

Oils and waxes are the best products to use to take care of wood or stone floors. Always use natural oils, such as linseed, or blends of oils derived from plants.

Top
PERFECT DRAWER

The wooden chests of drawers that were once a common feature of lawyers' offices make a stylish and practical addition to a study or workroom.

Bottom left
OLD AND NEW TOGETHER

Although the color of the wood gives this cupboard a classical look, the rounded metal handles and the way in which the doors open bring it completely up to date.

Bottom right
FLOOR-TO-CEILING DOORS

Both the wardrobe unit and the floor have been made from pale beech. Everything here is understated, including the hole pulls for handles. In a dressing room or small bedroom, this unit could be made into a walk-in closet with a mirror, to make the room seem larger.

Right
SYMMETRY WITH LINES

The symmetry of the doors and drawer fronts gives a classical appearance. Pale birch and a slightly darker hardwood have been used together.

Classical style for cabinets

There never seems to be enough cabinet space. Try to make existing cabinets part of the **decorative elements** of your home. Perhaps you can find an interesting example with a history from an antique or junk shop. Alternatively, you may prefer cabinets that are unique for a different reason, because they are custom-made. If they are of the right design, these cabinets will **form an intrinsic part of the style of the room.**

METALLIC PAINT FOR AN EXTRA DIMENSION

Furniture and accessories can be made to look very nice with metallic paint. Most well-known manufacturers produce their own metallic paints, but for small details, modeller's paints can be used. Even dull radiators can be enlivened with metallic paint, turning them from functional but unattractive items into decorative elements. Before using spray paint, completely remove the old paint, then treat the radiator with metal primer. This can then be sprayed over.

NICELY WORN

Gold leaf was traditionally used to decorate furniture, but, unfortunately, it was very easily damaged. As a result, few intact examples survive. However, the distressed look is back in vogue. A similar effect can be achieved by painting a layer of colored undercoat onto the furniture, followed by a coat of gold paint. This is then rubbed lightly with sandpaper to remove some of the gold and reveal glimpses of the color beneath.

Left
MIRROR FROM THE PAST
With their embellished frames intact, antique mirrors give a real period feel to the home. This 'butler's mirror' was used by staff to keep a discreet eye open for the needs of their master and his guests.

Top right
GLITTERING CURLICUES AND ORNAMENTATION
Furniture can be decorated with gold paint, but gold leaf is still used for picture frames.

Center right
ILLUMINATED STARS ON THE CEILING
This lamp was found in an antique shop but is actually a replica of a Moorish lantern. Similar lamps can be found in shops selling asian artifacts.

Bottom right
HEAT SOURCE
This radiator looks warm and inviting thanks to its color. Painting antique radiators in gold or bronze is an easy way of smartening them up.

Gold brings warmth

It was traditional to decorate picture frames with **gold leaf** to help give the appearance of a classical interior. In the new classical style, it is more a question of using gold **to provide warmth rather than to convey riches**. For those who want to do the real thing, there are courses in gilding. However, wonders can be performed with **spray cans of gold paint.**

COLORED UNITS

These simple kitchen units
are made from birch plywood.
Their rich look comes from an
unusual violet-gray stain that is
close to slate in color. Wood
stains are available in many
colors, in either transparent or
opaque finishes.

New Classical 114

The Grand Café style in the kitchen

The ambience of a Parisian café with the clink of glasses and china, relaxing music playing in the background and a tasteful decor can be recreated in your own kitchen. Use materials such as wood, terrazzo and stone, with details in metal for a professional touch. Add **creamy white china** with simple but elegant lines, and **stainless steel kitchen utensils.** The result is neat, classical and stylish.

COLLECTING PORCELAIN

Different shades of creamy white can be a feast for the eyes. Provided you choose designs that are similar, an entire dinner service can be assembled from second-hand china bought from different garage sales, flea markets and junk shops. The final collection will be unique.

HANDY AND ATTRACTIVE

Where the kitchen cabinets are on view in an open dining-room/kitchen, they will be more readily incorporated into the design of the room if a strip of material that complements the doors is placed along the edge of the countertop.

Top left
CREAMY PORCELAIN

Simple white china in creamy tones looks good against the warm tones of wood. Most manufacturers of fine china, such as Wedgwood, offer plain white dinner services.

Center left
ALL EYES ON THE OVEN

An oven as attractive as this deserves to be placed where it can be seen. The cupboard doors are smooth and plain and fill the entire space from floor to countertop, which is flush with the doors, so only the oven front stands out.

Bottom left
TO HAND

A row of small drawers near the stovetop is handy, and not just for cooking spoons and knives. If they are deep enough, they can hold jars of herbs and spices. Place the name of the herb or spice on the lid and you will easily be able to find what you need.

Right
FUTURE CLASSIC

Heat-resistant glass surrounds this stovetop. Although the plain plaster wall can still be seen, the glass makes the corner both practical and modern.

Personal style, classically done

FREE-STANDING KITCHEN APPLIANCES

Cooking appliances may be built into kitchen cabinets for a streamlined effect but they are also available as free-standing equipment to be placed between the cabinets, as shown on the facing page.

Top left
CLASSICAL WORKING KITCHEN

Modern kitchen equipment is placed among made-to-order cabinets built in inexpensive materials. There is a welcoming informality about this kitchen and it is clear that the family spends a great deal of time here.

Top right
NUANCES IN GRAY

This kitchen proves that gray can be radiantly bright. Extra warmth and interest can be given to terrazzo worktops with the addition of colored stone, mother-of-pearl or glass.

Bottom left
BEAUTIFUL DOWN TO THE LAST DETAIL

Quality is a feature of classical interiors. In this kitchen, wood, stainless steel and glass have been harmoniously combined.

Bottom right
GENUINE ZINC

Nineteenth-century Parisian bars featured tables and dressers covered in zinc, and these items may still be found in junk and antique shops. If you are really lucky, you might even find an authentic cork remover from the same period. The glasses are thick and robust to evoke a café atmosphere.

Top and bottom left

FOLLOWING OLD EXAMPLES

These classical window latches can be found in older houses, although seldom on every window. Replica replacements are, fortunately, now available.

Center left

BLACKBOARD

In the black-and-white kitchen, the perfect decoration for the back of the kitchen door or the utility room is blackboard paint. The surface, which can be written on and then wiped clean, is ideal for shopping lists.

Below left

FUN WITH LINES

By placing tiles vertically along the wall instead of horizontally, a border can be created. The black grouting contrasts with the plain white tiles, evoking a sense of the past.

Right

GRAPHIC DETAILS

Old prints and silhouettes are a rich source for many designers, as shown on these curtains. Should you want to design your own, there are copying services that will duplicate images onto fabric for you relatively cheaply.

The basic combination

Black and white will always make a striking combination in the home. **Graphic effects** work particularly well in these colors, which makes designing and living with black and white enormous fun. Sometimes the simplest styles can have the greatest potential.

THOUGHTFUL WITH TILES
The white wall tiling has been broken at waist height with blocks of black for dramatic effect. The mirror above the vanity unit reflects the result on the opposite wall, creating a sense of space. A filing cabinet is a novel idea for storage.

MOISTURE PROBLEMS WITH MIRRORS
To prevent mirrors being spoiled by moisture, either fix them a little away from the wall, so that a small cavity is formed, or fix them into the wall so that no moisture can seep behind. For a guaranteed condensation-free reflection, install a heated mirror.

CHAPTER 4

Color & Contrast

The importance of color

Color is the most important element of interior design, and a home decorated around a color scheme will have a strong and personal style. Color can create a feeling of space and breathe life into a room. It can affect the way in which light is reflected and so alter the mood of a room. By choosing the color of unbleached linen or red earth for the walls, bright green and yellow checks for the tablecloth, or perhaps a blue vase for the table, the effect you create will be stunning.

From mood setting to visual surprises

4 CONTENTS

Color & Contrast

THE PALETTE OF COLOR AND CONTRAST

Rainbow colors, from sunset yellow to brilliant green, suit bright, contemporary interiors. Although muted shades are not as appropriate to this style of decorating, you could try deeper, more saturated pastel colors, evoking tropical islands with their vibrant flowers, fruit and clear, blue sea.

CHOOSING THE RIGHT COLOR

Paint colors can be mixed to your individual requirements: in certain stores, scanners will analyze any color you like – whether from a favorite fabric sample or a magazine photograph – and then work out the correct color formula for you on the computer. Paint colors from the past are also available in heritage hues, if you are looking for a color with historical associations.

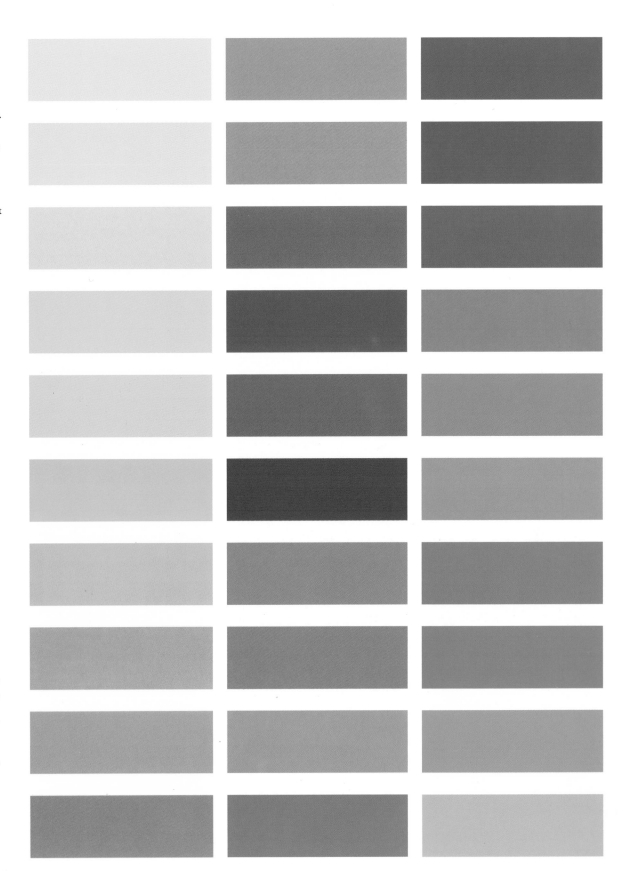

Color as inspiration

There are many ways of **living with color** – in an understated way with subdued colors, or exuberantly with plenty of contrast. Your choice of color mirrors your personality and determines whether you feel at home in a room. Color is also a means by which a specific style can be attained or a mood created. All that matters is your **personal preference**.

YELLOW, THE COLOR OF SUN AND SUMMER
White will probably soon be overtaken by yellow as the most popular color for walls. Yellow is very versatile: not only is it the color of the sun, but it can also help to conjure up an oriental atmosphere. Here, a deep, sunset yellow has been combined with a warm red sofa, a table from India and decorative accessories to evoke the mood of the East.

COMBINING COLORS
By collecting color
samples in combinations
that you like, you will
get a clear idea of
your favourite colors.
If you want to create
the mood of a
particular country,
it helps to use an
association of ideas.
To create the mood
of India, for example,
use the colors of
saris and spices as
a starting point.

This small room, on a different level from the adjacent dining room, originally had another entrance. Now the rooms are linked and also share a color scheme. The yellow harmonizes beautifully with the pine floor, while the fuchsia of the chair is the main focus of color.

WALLPAPER VERSUS PAINT
The advantage of wallpaper is that you can get an immediate impression of how it will look before you hang it. With paint the effect is delayed while you wait for it to dry. It is also influenced by any underlying color and reflected light. The advantage of paint is that it is easier to change than wallpaper, and a beautiful result can be achieved quickly, even by those who are less skilled at decorating.

Adapting the available space

SPACIOUS EFFECT
The impression of height in a room can be influenced by the choice of color. Here the sloping ceiling above the door has been painted white, distinguishing it from the wall, and making the sloping area seem less oppressive.

Vibrant colors for furnishing fabrics

**COLORS FROM
A PAINTER'S PALETTE**
Furnishing fabrics in vibrant
colors, such as lime green,
cobalt and sunflower yellow,
employ every possible motif,
from squares through tie-dye
to flowers or decorative letters.

One space, one color

Choosing one color for one space is very **classical.** Traditionally, this was common practice in cottages, and it is now coming back into fashion: a blue room, a red room, and so on. **Color affects the light,** which is why north-facing rooms are often painted in warm earth colors, while blue, sea-green and lilac shades are preferred for rooms facing south.

NATURAL COLORS
Exploiting the natural tones of metal and wood can be most effective. Wood often has a yellow or brown tinge, while that of stainless steel, zinc and aluminium is blue, gray or lilac. The surrounding colors can be finely tuned to match.

Top left
DISPLAY CABINET IN DIFFERENT COLORS

The front of this wooden display cabinet, found in an antique shop, has been painted reddish-brown. For the back panel, an emerald green was chosen to offset the white porcelain and give the cabinet an impression of greater depth.

Top right
ADVANTAGES OF A DADO

Dado panelling brings various benefits: electric cables can be hidden away and the lower part of the wall can easily be wiped clean, which is useful if you have small children. Buy ready-made panels from builders supply, or design your own using plywood and wooden mouldings.

Bottom left
COOL WITH WARMTH

A staircase and landing can be painted in bold, vibrant colors simply because you spend very little time there and will not be overwhelmed by them. In this example, the strong, warm red compensates for the cool light and enhances the color of the wood.

Bottom right
TRADITIONAL COLORS FOR THE BATHROOM

A combination of blue and white is the traditional 'fresh' color scheme for a bathroom. The mosaic tiles on the wall are made of glass and have a watercolor-like translucence.

Top left
DECORATIONS FOR MORE THAN JUST THE TABLE

A vase of flowers, some earthenware, a candlestick or a dish need not be regarded simply as decorations for the table; they can also be used to great effect on a sideboard or dresser. The slender forms and strong colors used here draw the eye immediately.

Center left
KEEP IT SIMPLE

Flowers have long been the traditional accompaniment to an elegant dinner service, white, starched napkins and beautifully presented meal. A single bloom laid on a serving dish forms a simple yet stunning centerpiece.

Bottom left
ALTERNATIVE TO TILES

Paint is a viable alternative to wall tiles above the countertop. Painting the plaster in the color of your choice is cheap as well as quick and simple to change. A final coat of varnish makes the wall waterproof and easier to clean. To avoid scorching, make sure that the stovetop is not set too close to the wall. An Italian mood has been created in this kitchen with terracotta walls, white units, beech worktops and a classical checkered floor.

Casual dining

Setting time aside in our busy lives to **dine with family and friends** is becoming increasingly important. Sitting around a table together creates friendly, intimate moments and strengthens our bonds. The dining-room therefore deserves **warm and inviting colors** to evoke a comfortable atmosphere that encourages conversation.

SMALL DETAIL,
BIG IMPACT

The reddish-orange wall –
actually just two strips of color
– creates a cozy atmosphere that
is enhanced by the colorful
tableware. The original wooden
panelling of the mansard ceiling
was replaced with replica boards
for an authentic look.

WOOD STAIN in soft watercolor tints can soften the appearance of flooring in south-facing rooms.

LARGE CARPET TILES, when laid diagonally, create the look of an Italian mansion.

LAMINATED FLOORING comes in various wood finishes and a wide range of colors.

GLASS MOSAIC TILES can be laid quickly in blocks of 12 x 12in (30 x 30cm). Given that a large number of colors are available, you can achieve almost any effect you wish.

QUARRY TILES can be bought in their traditional undecorated finish as well as in numerous colors and designs for creating patterns.

CARPETS are available in some outstanding colors. Different-colored carpets can be cut and laid in pieces to create a striped effect.

Far right

COMBINING various types of floor-covering can create a sense of division between areas. Here traditional floor tiles are used in the hallway, but warm, natural sisal has been laid in the adjoining room. The contrast of vivid and tranquil colors, as well as smooth and hard surfaces, produces unexpected but delightful results.

CLEANING QUARRY TILES
General stains can be mopped up with a liquid abrasive cleaner, while white patches can be treated with a vinegar solution.

Be daring and combine different types of flooring, and let them meet at doorways to **emphasize the contrast.** Sisal that runs into a parquet floor places soft and hard side by side. Let the floor covering continue part way into the next room for an unusual effect. Make use of the fact that the floor is either the **greatest reflector or absorber of light,** which can influence your choice of color scheme greatly. Materials and color are your tools; be sure to use them well.

Contrast in color and materials on the floor

TILES TO YOUR OWN DESIGN
Artisan tile-makers will produce tiles in your chosen colors and design.

Left
NATURAL HARMONY OF BEECH WITH YELLOW
The yellow in the tiles finds an echo in the warmth of the beech kitchen cabinets. The tiles were made-to-order.

Right
COLORFUL KITCHEN, ITALIAN-STYLE
Wood and metal seem poles apart, yet they harmonize beautifully. The range and oven find an echo in the stainless steel wall-covering, and the bases of the orange wooden cupboards are also finished with a strip of stainless steel.

Far right
SPACE-SAVER
Practical shelves can be created in the smallest of spaces. Open shelves that are narrow yet deep are an attractive way of storing china and glassware.

Nostalgia with high-tech

A colorful home requires a complementary kitchen. Since the predominant theme is color, you are therefore completely free to use or combine any decorating style that stikes your fancy. The result can be absolutely wonderful, from sober wood with rustic tiles to steel with hot, sunny colors. **In today's kitchen there is room for both high-tech and nostalgia.**

WOOD FLOORS FOR THE KITCHEN

Smooth cabinet doors are coming back into fashion, often in conjunction with stainless steel. Using a warm material such as wood for the floor prevents a clinical look. Varnished floors soon develop a worn patch near the work surface, and it is difficult to revarnish just a part of the floor; for this reason it is better to impregnate and treat wood floors with wax, which can easily be touched up. The best choices are hardwoods, but avoid oak because water will stain it.

New uses for tried and true materials

Top left

CURVES IN THE KITCHEN

Beech is the perfect material
for kitchen counters because it
is hygienic and fairly water-
resistant. Rounded-off edges
and corners are far more
attractive than right angles,
and can be machined to order.

Top right

MEDITERRANEAN TIME

The owner of this kitchen
took her inspiration from the
Mediterranean. The simple
beauty of the white tiles has
a clean, contemporary appeal,
and a note of variation was
added with a border of tiles
laid vertically. The minimalist
clock fits the scheme of things.

Bottom left

CLEVERLY USED

To add textural interest to the
ceiling, the previously white
beams were roughly sanded to
allow the color of the wood to
show through. Given that there
is rarely enough storage space
in a kitchen, it is a good idea
to put any unused space to
work – including that above
your head. You will never
again have to hunt for a pan
deep in the back of a cupboard.

Bottom right

DRAWERS ON WHEELS

New ideas are entering the
kitchen. This transparent
plastic trolley, with its stainless
steel frame and four deep
drawers, is easy to use as well
as a pleasure to look at.

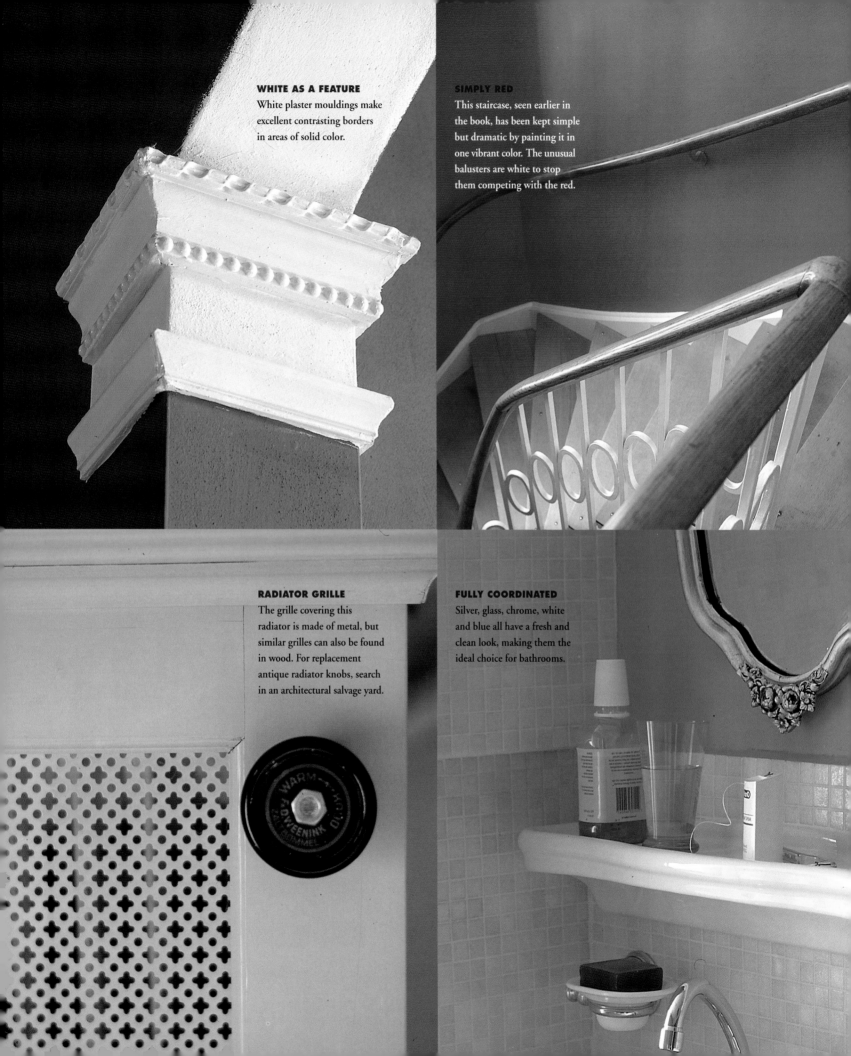

WHITE AS A FEATURE

White plaster mouldings make
excellent contrasting borders
in areas of solid color.

SIMPLY RED

This staircase, seen earlier in
the book, has been kept simple
but dramatic by painting it in
one vibrant color. The unusual
balusters are white to stop
them competing with the red.

RADIATOR GRILLE

The grille covering this
radiator is made of metal, but
similar grilles can also be found
in wood. For replacement
antique radiator knobs, search
in an architectural salvage yard.

FULLY COORDINATED

Silver, glass, chrome, white
and blue all have a fresh and
clean look, making them the
ideal choice for bathrooms.

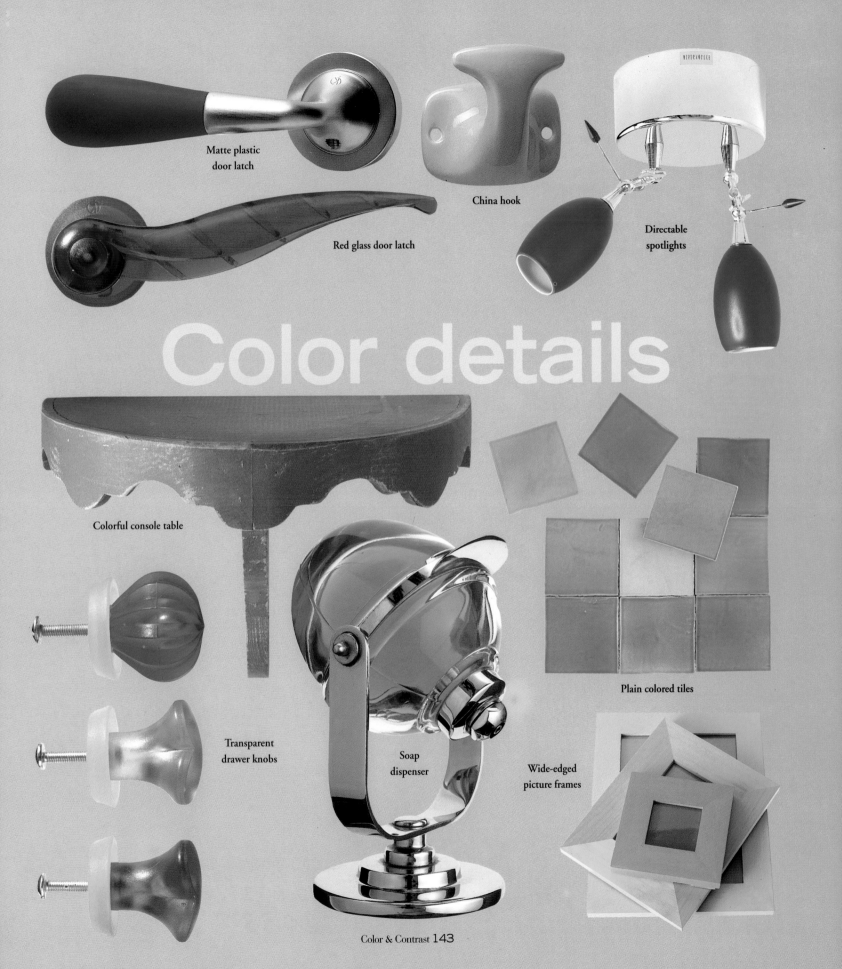

Matte plastic
door latch

China hook

Directable
spotlights

Red glass door latch

Color details

Colorful console table

Transparent
drawer knobs

Soap
dispenser

Plain colored tiles

Wide-edged
picture frames

Color & Contrast 143

CLASSICAL MOTIF
The sun motif has a classical style that gives this bright and airy room a timeless charm.

Summery bedrooms

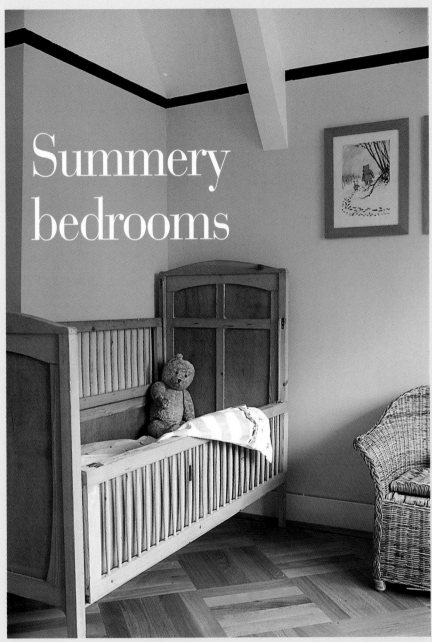

Left
NOSTALGIC WALL
A border of paint or wallpaper at picture-rail height helps to create a more intimate feeling in a room with a high ceiling.

Right
DISGUISED DOOR
A doorway that is no longer used can be hidden behind a cabinet; alternatively it can be used as a frame for a new cabinet. This mobile shelf unit was built to the precise measurements of the doorway. Baskets on the shelves in place of drawers are useful for carrying laundry.

More fabric is generally used in the bedroom than anywhere else in the home. This offers plenty of opportunity for creating **fantastic effects** with bold designs, especially as a bed cover can quite easily, and relatively cheaply, be replaced. It is a good idea to **paint the walls** in just one color, choosing a shade that stands out. Consider **fresh lime green,** for example.

Top left
BED LINEN IN RESERVE

Bed linen that complements your bedroom color scheme provides the perfect finishing touch. You might consider buying even more than you need just in case the design is discontinued by the time the linen needs replacing.

Center left
BRIGHT COLORS

Lightweight blankets in bright colors are perfect for late summer when it is too hot for a duvet but too cool for sheets.

Bottom left
SQUARES, FLOWERS AND STRIPES

Lots of pillows and generous bed covers in squares, stripes and brightly colored flowers make a bedroom inviting.

Right
TROPICAL NIGHTS

The mosquito net brings to mind distant lands. As well as being useful on hot summer nights, it also lends a romantic air to the bedroom. During the day it can be twisted into a rope and lightly tied into a loop. It can then be let down at night in one easy movement.

Bed linen with a new look

IDEAS FOR COLOR
The combination of white with multicolored floral designs creates a summery bedroom all year round. The old-fashioned bedstead adds a rustic touch.

YESTERDAY'S BED, TODAY'S COMFORT
Old-style iron bedsteads, complete with good quality bases, are enjoying a revival.

BE DARING

Bold elements, such as the humorous painting and extra large floor tiles, enliven this hallway. The second-hand sideboard has been painted a strong green to contrast with the wall and checkered floor.

Top right
PRETTY PICTURE

Still-lifes occur spontaneously in the home, inspiring color combinations that you might never have considered.

Bottom left
FLORAL INSPIRATION

Flowers have been a source of inspiration for artists through the ages and for all who love color in their home. Flowers often have intense colors that vary in tone from petal to petal. This effect can be copied with emulsion paint and fabrics.

Right
CONTRASTING DESIGN

Although the pattern of this throw is in complete contrast to that of the sofa, a delightful color balance is created.

If you choose strong colors, it is advisable to keep the furniture **classic, timeless and simple,** so that the colors themselves can play the leading role. Accessories are ideal for trying out **new thoughts and ideas** because you can experiment with them until the desired effect is achieved.

Classic shapes
in color

Walls that come alive

THE STYLE OF AN OLD HOUSE

The look of an old house can sometimes be recreated with colorwashes – a technique widely used in new houses to give a feeling of age. The walls can be made less smooth by adding special finishes.

Top left
THE COTTAGE LOOK

Adding texture to a wall is easy with a colorwash; a few layers of paint will produce an ageing effect. The door has also been treated with a colorwash.

Top right
SPONGING, DRAGGING AND DABBING

The character and texture of a surface can be influenced by the use of sponges, cloths or wide brushes. The way in which the paint is applied also has an effect, whether you use circles, broad sweeps or light dabs. A radiator and pipes painted the same color as the wall will appear less obtrusive.

Bottom left and right
COLORWASH AS BACKGROUND

The relaxed and informal look of a colorwash lends itself to small bedrooms and casual corners with collections of photographs, postcards or prints. Tints such as yellow or orange create an Italian feel.

Right
DUTCH INSPIRATION

The inspiration for this room, with its red-and-white check armchair against a wall covered with ultramarine colorwash paper, comes from traditional Dutch interiors.

Far right
AN IDEAL CONTRAST

Soft orange colorwashed walls are the perfect contrast to the wooden basin surround.

COLORWASH: BOOKS THAT TELL YOU HOW
Colorwashing is fun to do, but if you have never tried it before, there are many books about special painting and decorating techniques that will give you all the guidance you need.

Colorwash means, quite simply, washing with colors. **Walls come to life** with this technique and rooms get a **lived-in, rustic character.** Colorwashing starts with a light undercoat to which the color is applied with a wide distemper brush. The paint is then either rubbed in circles with a wet flannel wrapped in cloth, or dabbed with a sponge. For a **powdery effect** you can apply diluted white paint over a coat of color. Special colorwash paints are available from paint stores, but ordinary emulsion works perfectly well. **Bold experimentation produces the best results.**

Moving away from classic white

Glass mosaic tiles are available in many styles and colors. Their translucent properties give the bathroom a cool, aquatic feel. Waterproofing bathroom walls is an alternative to tiling, as it opens up more possibilities for decoration. **Wooden panelling** can also look very attractive in a bathroom.

MAKING THE MOST OF EXISTING FEATURES

Making use of existing features can deliver very pleasing results. The original, glass-fronted cupboard was kept during the remodeling of this bathroom, and in the new layout, there is space beneath it for the bath.

TRADITIONAL DETAILS

This unusual vanity unit has been made by cutting out the top of an old table to take a chrome or stainless steel basin. The finishing touch is the traditional-style faucet. The wood has been protected with waterproofing paint.

ANTIQUE-STYLE BATHROOM FITTINGS

Reproduction fixtures, faucets and fittings are widely available, providing the finishing touches to a classical bathroom.

Top left
SIMPLE FEATURES SET THE STYLE

Style can be created without grand gestures. A single, old-fashioned faucet set in the wall above a marble basin with a chrome drainpipe are the small details that suggest both refinement and grandeur.

Center left
CLASSIC FEATURES

Antique objects can dictate a look. To display this French mirror, the mosaic stops part way up the wall, and the remaining plaster is decorated in a dreamy shade of lavender.

Bottom left
BEHIND FALSE WALLS

False walls can make bathroom improvements easier as pipes can be hidden away behind them. If the walls stop at half the height of the bathroom, they provide handy shelving for lotions and potions.

Mediterranean summer hues

Far left

LOVE AFFAIR WITH WARMER CLIMES

Holidays in warmer climates give you the opportunity to see what can be achieved with tile designs. They can be delightful in the home, especially in the bathroom. The pattern on this floor is repeated on the wall.

Left

THINKING BIG

A washbasin surround can be made from a wide range of materials, including wood, stone and terrazzo. This top is made of concrete, with black toner added to the mix. On another base it would seem far too big, but the generous size of the basin, the strong cobalt blue of the tiles, combined with the sturdy supports, make for an unusual, stylish result.

Practicalities

Renovation to repairs

5 CONTENTS

Planning and preparation

Many look back on their first efforts at do-it-yourself and declare: 'The next time I'm going to do this the right way.' The things you ought to know before you start usually come to light only after you have encountered the problems. For example, what to do with all those wires from the television, telephone and lamps that are running across the living room floor? How to cope with blistering in the newly painted ceiling? Why won't the new fireplace draw smoke properly?

The final chapter of this book therefore provides basic information on practical matters related to making a home, and tips on how to deal with possible problems. It is intended not as a complete do-it-yourself guide (although it does include a mini-course in painting and decorating) but more as inspiration for an important stage in your home-making: the planning and preparation before the work gets underway.

Buying a home

Buying a home is one of the most exciting times in life, but making the right decision requires some careful thinking as well as enthusiasm. Choosing the right property for you depends on understanding your living requirements and your aspirations. Home purchase often coincides with other significant changes in life, such as a marriage or a new relationship, or the arrival of a baby or other addition to the household. These changes may impose previously unanticipated demands on the home, which need to be taken into consideration. Buying a house is considered to be an extremely stressful undertaking, with anxieties over financial matters, communicating with contractors and vendors, and coordinating the actual move itself. Try to remain calm: The result will be worth it.

DECIDING WHAT YOU NEED

Start by asking yourself some basic questions to help you form an idea of what you are really looking for: How many bedrooms and communal rooms do you want? Is a garden important to you or will it be a burden to maintain? Do you want to live in a city, town or village environment? Will access via stairs be a problem or do you need a property on one level? Do you want a single- or multi-story property? Do you want to buy a new property or an older but well-maintained one? Do you want to design your own living space, and would therefore find rebuilding, remodeling, converting or building anew a more flexible and cost-effective option? Will the upheaval of any remodeling work be an inconvenience to you or to any other member of the household?

PERSONAL BUDGET

A good place to start is to work out how much you can afford to pay. For this purpose it is sensible to work out your personal budget. To do this, you should set out your income and expenditures in two columns next to each other. Income includes salary, bonuses and other fixed payments to you. On the opposite side there are three types of expenditures: the fixed costs (including insurance, local taxes, energy costs and utlities such as telephone) which are paid at set intervals; household costs, for example food, clothing, repairs to house and garden, and entertainment; and third, major expenditure for things like furniture or vacations. A quick way to get an overview of these costs is to look at your bank statements for the previous year. Most lenders will help you to assess your cash flow and budget, often with the aid of a financial planner or loan officer.

MORTGAGES

Once you have an idea of your living costs, you can start the process of looking for a mortgage. Banks, mortgage brokers, real estate agents and other lenders can provide you with more information. With their advice, and by asking extensive questions about the current interest rate, payments, and terms and conditions, you can decide which is the most suitable mortgage for you. If your new home is likely to need improvements or repairs, ask whether these costs can be included in your mortgage. Home

> **FINANCE FIRST**
> Before you rush out to buy the home of your dreams, think very carefully about the financial implications. Affordability is a big factor in choosing the right home.

loans are available to help buy properties in need of rebuilding, converting or for buying land and building anew.

It is a good idea to leave yourself some financial breathing space. If you borrow the maximum permissible amount you could find yourself unable to pay for work that you had not anticipated but which, nevertheless, is essential. You may also be vulnerable to any increases in mortgage interest rates.

A READY-MADE HOME

If you do not want to get involved in anything other than furnishing or decorating your home, then you are likely to want to find a property that is either new, or in very good structural condition. The price is likely to reflect the fact that very little or no work is required – new properties may even carry a price premium.

REBUILDING

If you intend to have a greater influence on the interior design and layout of your home, then you will probably find it more cost-effective to buy a property already requiring structural repairs, as the price will reflect the amount of work that needs to be done. Properties in need of modernization, repair or renovation are a good option if you do not want to take on too much work and too big a mortgage, but want to stamp your identity on your home. This can still be a good way to get more home for your money, especially if you are prepared to get involved in some of the work yourself on a do-it-yourself basis. Common requirements are the installation of new plumbing and wiring, new fixtures and kitchen units, and repairs to the basic structure. It is usually relatively easy to move internal partition walls, if you want to rearrange the room layout, or to remove them altogether. Sections of floor on an upper level may even be removed if you want to create double height areas, and staircases too can be moved.

Look for properties that still have many of their period features intact, like original doors and windows, flooring, mouldings and fireplaces. These can be restored or stripped and refinished and can make wonderful features. Do not be put off by the condition of existing decoration or furnishing, or the state of the garden, all of which can easily be changed. Look for properties that offer the potential for additions or attic conversion. This extra accommodation can add value to your home, but check with the local authorities about any building restrictions before buying.

CONVERSION

Some of the most unusual homes have been built in structures that were formerly used for some other purpose. The ever increasing change from outlying farmlands to industrial-based economies has left behind a large number of former agricultural buildings, such as old barns and mills, often in idyllic rural locations.

POTENTIAL FOR CONVERSION

In many countries, some churches and other places of worship are vacant and falling into disrepair. Although sometimes difficult to convert, especially if set in consecrated ground, the results can be spectacular.

Other buildings that may offer potential space in which to create your home include old schools, offices, warehouses, watermills, lighthouses and even old jails. Among the more unusual choices for conversion have been an old fire house, a general store, a boathouse, a sailmaker's loft, and a soap factory.

These can frequently be bought extremely cheaply, although converting them into homes or apartments that meet today's exacting building codes can be fairly expensive. Concurrent with this migration from the countryside to the cities, there has also been a decline in large-scale industry and a tendency to relocate businesses from expensive city offices to much cheaper out-of-town sites. This has left a number of warehouses, factories and other former industrial buildings abandoned. Some are sufficiently small to form a single dwelling, but most are large buildings that are spilt up into individual units by property developers and then bought by private individuals. Sold as a shell, such buildings can present an exciting opportunity to design a home from scratch within an existing structure, in an otherwise completely built-up area, often in the center of a town or city. Such spaces can often be light and airy, lending themselves to some very innovative modern designs. On the downside, they can be difficult and expensive to heat, due to their size.

Before purchasing any property for conversion into a home, it is essential to get a clear idea of the costs that will be involved by commissioning an inspection and consulting a building professional, such as an architect, building surveyor or structural engineer. They will be able to assess the suitability of the structure for your intended use and will also be able to help assess the cost of bringing water, electricity, telephone and other essential services to the property.

BUILDING YOUR OWN HOME

Where land for building is available, designing and building a new house from scratch offers the greatest freedom to create your own personally designed living environment. Providing you comply with the local design and building codes, which you should check before buying a site, you can create whatever sort of home you want, modern or traditional, with a room plan arranged exactly as you want. This can be a very cost-effective way of creating an individual home, as building a new property is often less expensive per square foot of living space than converting or rebuilding an existing structure. For further advice, consult a professional designer such as an architect or surveyor.

LOCATION

Location is one of the most important factors to consider when buying or building a home. As well as thinking about where you would like to live, think of the practicalities such as proximity to friends and family, work, shops and schools. Travelling may not be a problem today, but commuting is becoming increasingly time-consuming and expensive as the number of cars per capita increases.

CHECKING THE PROPERTY

Before purchasing any property, make sure that you arrange for an appropriately qualified expert to undertake a survey to assess the suitability of the property for your intended use. Even new buildings may have faults, and it pays to be aware of what these are before parting with your money.

If you are planning rebuilding or conversion work, a detailed survey is absolutely vital. The professional inspector, usually a surveyor, will prepare a report that will detail the structural condition of the property, and any repairs that are required, possibly with an indication of the likely cost of the work. The surveyor's report can also be used to gain estimates from builders for the work. Any information discovered during the inspection can be used to renegotiate the purchase price with the seller. Before appointing any professional, make sure you take references and check that they are appropriately insured and a member of the relevant trade association. Agree on the price and details in writing of any work you want them to undertake before the work commences, and ensure that each of you keeps a signed copy.

CAREFUL BUDGETING

If you are planning extensive renovation or conversion work, or are building your own home, prepare your budget carefully by talking to builders and professionals. Allow for alternative accommodation while work is underway, professionals' fees, connection of services such as water, gas and electricity and a 10% contingency amount.

Planning the interior

Everything seems possible in a new property or one that is being extensively renovated or remodelled. It is great fun visiting builders supply, fabric and furniture shops and deciding how to furnish and decorate. Although it may be easier to decide on some of these things after you have lived in your home for a while, it is sensible to work out from the outset what style of furniture will fit and what sizes the various pieces can be.

Do you yearn to buy new furniture even before the construction work is finished, or have you not yet decided how to furnish your new home? To help you with the dimensions and proportions of the rooms and possible furnishings, it is a good idea to make a plan of the floor area. It will help greatly with deciding how to use the space in the home. A scale of 1:20 gives a good impression (one full inch equals twenty inches in reality). Try using graph paper – the grid makes drawing any plans much easier.

REMOVING WALLS

Once you have a plan, it is easy to try out lots of different ideas, moving or removing the walls or adding extra space until you reach a room layout that suits your lifestyle and aspirations. In reality, a builder or architect will advise you whether it is safe to remove a particular wall or whether openings can be created. New walls can easily be constructed from sheetrock and wood studs or with lightweight concrete blocks. Archways can be created using special metal forms which can be plastered over.

ARRANGING THE FURNITURE

Use a similar 1:20 plan for arranging the furniture. Draw each piece of furniture as seen from above to the same scale and cut out the drawings. Now you can move the paper furniture around as often as you need to see how your real furniture will fit in the new home. Try to visualize the end result and bear in mind the space needed to walk around the room and between furniture. Do not forget to allow for the space that is needed to open doors and windows (if these open inwards) and allow enough room to pass by without bumping into them.

DIVIDING WITH FURNITURE

Rooms can be divided with furniture as well as with walls. A sideboard or dresser, a dining table or free-standing storage units can all be used to section off parts of a room (see illustration top far right). A more spacious effect is achieved if the cupboard does not reach higher than 20 inches from the ceiling, so that the ceiling is seen to continue. This is particularly important in smaller living areas. The right height for cabinets against the walls needs to be related to the distance between them and the rest of the furniture and also to the width of the room. A tall bookcase less than 10 feet in front of a sofa can seem intimidating. In such a case it is better to place the bookcase to the side or behind the field of view and to have a lower cabinet in front of you.

DETERMINING SPACE: THE FLOOR TO CEILING HEIGHT

The floor and ceiling play an important role in the spatial arrangement of the home. The finish and color of the flooring and walls have an influence, but more important are their heights and levels. To create a more intimate area with a large room, an area of raised or sunken floor or a change in ceiling levels can be used as a division, without losing the sense of spaciousness.

DESIGNING IN 3-D

Many interior designers prefer to work in three dimensions rather than on a flat piece of paper. The simplest way to do this is to make a small-scale model of the living space and furniture items from cardboard. This is considerably easier than it sounds – more like making a small dolls' house – and can reveal many problems that are not immediately apparent when working in only two dimensions. An even easier way of visualizing your ideas in 3-D is with the help of a home or interior design program on a personal computer. Most households now have access to a personal computer, and home and interior design software packages are inexpensive and simple to use.

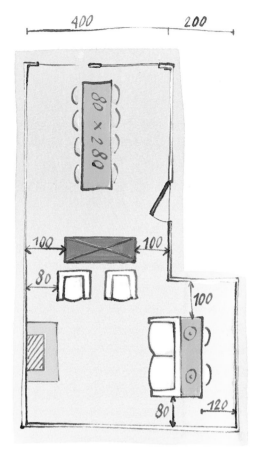

Left

A small wall set at an angle to one of the main walls can form a discrete study area, as well as providing some useful extra shelving.

Right

A cupboard between two parts of a room creates two separate areas – one for dining and the other for relaxing – and provides more storage space.

Annotated measurements are in centimeters: 90cm = 3ft

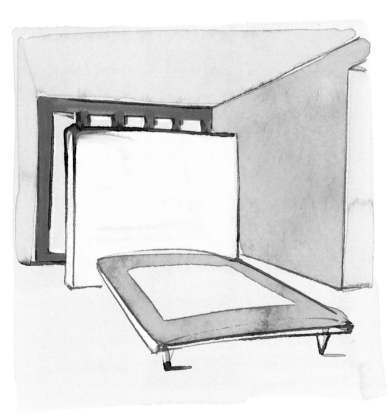

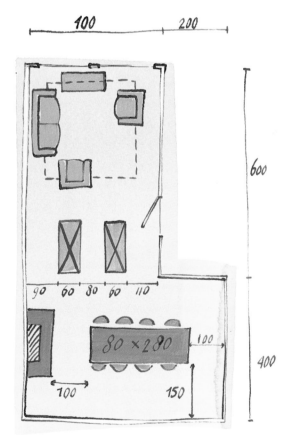

Left

Partitions that do not reach to the ceiling make a room feel more spacious. Here a dressing area has been provided behind the bed.

Right

For more light in the room, two cabinets can be arranged in parallel formation, as in a library. The necessary circulation space within and between the two separate areas is maintained.

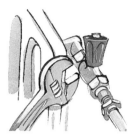

Turn the water off and undo the nut.

Connect the valve to the radiator and pipe.

Fix the knob on the valve and adjust it.

Installations

Installations in the home include the central heating and ventilation, electrical wiring, and plumbing. The installation of any of these has to comply with the building codes of your local area. These regulations may seem to be an obstacle to some of your more creative ideas, but they contribute greatly to safety in the home.

HOT WATER SYSTEM

Central heating systems that are separate from the hot water system are increasingly being replaced by combination hot water heaters that provide the central heating and provide hot water on demand. These are particularly appropriate for smaller properties, where the demand on heating and hot water is light. Larger households with two or more bathrooms may prefer some form of hot water storage, especially if baths are used, as demand may outstrip the boiler's ability to heat water. This may be a small 'side saddle' tank, added to a combination boiler, or a separate boiler and hot water tank.

The energy efficiency of your water heater will have a huge influence on your running costs, so consider investing in a condensing or other type of high efficiency model. Where the local water pressure is sufficient, an ordinary plumbing system may be appropriate, providing excellent flow rates without the need for

additional storage tanks or pumps. Such systems also eliminate the requirement for pumps on showers, as the pressure is already sufficient for a satisfying and exhilarating flow. Installing a hot water system yourself is possible, but make sure you know about the correct connection of the flow and return pipes, the distance apart they must be, and the connection of thermostatic valves (see left). These all have a major part to play in the efficiency of the system.

THE MOST POWERFUL SHOWER JET

The pressure of the shower jet will depend on two factors: the type of equipment installed and the flow rates and temperatures of the hot and cold water supply. Thermostatic shower mixers are available with manual temperature controls, which may need to be adjusted if the flow rate of hot or cold water varies because of demand elsewhere in the home. Showers with built-in thermostatic flow controls are also available; these

will adjust their own flow rate to maintain a constant, preselected temperature, regardless of changes in pressure. The hot water flow rate will depend on the type of heater and tank installed and the cold water flow rate that supplies it. If the pressure is inadequate for any reason, a pumped or power shower system should be installed.

BATH AND SHOWER USED TOGETHER

A shower uses about $1^{3}/_{4}$–$3^{1}/_{4}$ gallons (8–15 liters) of hot water per minute and the average bath about $3^{1}/_{4}$–$6^{1}/_{2}$ gallons (15–30 litres). A tank with a capacity of $17^{1}/_{2}$ gallons (80 litres) per minute is therefore necessary if both are to be used at once.

CHOOSING YOUR HEATING FUEL

Choosing which fuel to use to heat your home will depend on local availability, installation and running costs, convenience, and any evnironmental concerns that you may have.

THE ELECTRICAL WIRING

Should you decide to wire or rewire your home, remember that safety is of paramount importance. Each area has its own electrical codes and it is important first to find out what these are and then to comply with them. Before the electrical circuit can be

connected to the supply on new properties, it will have to be officially checked by the local electric company. For rebuilding or remodelling projects, ensure that the supply is switched off before starting any work. Electricity is particularly dangerous in rooms that become wet, i.e. kitchens and bathrooms, and so the rules on installation in these areas are very strict. It is possible to undertake wiring and rewiring on a do-it-yourself basis, and a diagram drawn to scale is very useful in creating a wiring plan. You can draw in all the switches and sockets you need in each room, plan your circuits and calculate how much wire is needed. If you want feature lighting, perhaps with different circuits for table, wall and ceiling lights, then plan it now.

SPECIAL COMPUTER CONNECTIONS

It is advisable to have a dedicated circuit for the power supply to a computer. This prevents interference from other equipment sharing the circuit. It is also worth installing a device that will protect the computer from fluctuations in the current which could damage the equipment.

Warm air

Cold air

Make sure that there is an adequate through flow of air when boxing in a radiator.

VENTILATION

Good ventilation is essential to prevent the build-up of condensation and moisture which may damage the components of the building. Ventilation should remove damp, stale air, and replace it with dry, fresh air from outside the building, thus creating a balance of air flow. Ventilation is particularly important in wet areas, such as the kitchen and bathrooms, and most areas now have strict rules to ensure that properties are adequately ventilated. Ventilation can also be used to extract smells and some allergens.

TYPES OF VENTILATION SYSTEMS

There are ducted and surface-mounted ventilation systems. The first type can be installed in tubular ducts, but this out-of-sight variety can usually only be installed during the early stages of building. Ventilation is provided by one of two methods: mechanical fans or using the principle of convection.

Wall-mounted ventilation systems are usually in the form of an extractor fan that can be connected to a light switch. Some models even continue working for a given length of time after the light has been switched off. These are highly suitable for bathrooms. There are also models with a humidity detector. These switch off only when the humidity has been reduced sufficiently.

Original detail

Those who chose an older house have chosen the charm and architecture of the past. Sometimes, however, such a house has been modernized and all the original features have been removed or hidden behind panelling. There are countless specialty suppliers of old building materials that can help you bring your home back to its original look. Alternatively, you can contact architectural salvage suppliers and try to find originals.

LEADED GLASS

If the leaded glass is missing, there are two ways to discover what used to be there. There may be houses in the vicinity that still have their leaded glass intact. Ask the owners if you may take photographs of it. Then you can ask a leaded glass craftsman to copy the design for you. If there are no examples to be found, perhaps a leaded glass studio can advise you on the style best suited to your home.

If you have a steady hand and are feeling ambitious, sign up for a course in leaded glass and make your own window.

It is somewhat different when the window needs to provide insulation or security. You can opt for new double glazing with leaded glass inserted between the panes. The studio will have contacts for this process. Another possibility is to install secondary glazing.

REMOVING OLD PAINT FINISHES

Panel doors or banisters with attractive spindles are often covered in layers of dirty old paint and/or varnish. You can clean them yourself, but if you use a scraper there is a strong possibility that you will damage fine moulding and detail, while sandpapering intricate designs can be very tiresome and not always satisfactory. Specialist contractors can remove all the layers of old paint, varnish and grime using a strong alkaline solution without damaging the details or harming the glue in the joints. Bear in mind that they cannot work at your home, so you will need to dismantle everything to take it to them. Windows can also be treated, although the glazing will have to be removed if it is held in place by putty rather than glazing beads, as the putty may be removed with the paint. The process is not cheap, and items may still require some cleaning afterwards. Before making a decision, make sure that the item is worth stripping.

MAKING A REPLICA

Sometimes an ornamental feature indoors or out is damaged or has bits missing, or one of a pair has vanished completely. Think of banister spindles, for instance, or decorative features on the exterior wall, or perhaps ornamental brackets supporting a beam or the ceiling. It may be possible to find an old replacement from a salvage yard, but in most cases it will be easier to find a new replacement. A wide range of replicas of period items are available from many suppliers, and these are likely to be a more cost-effective option than going for an original. If, however, your missing feature is very unusual, then you may need to have a replacement made especially, and there are companies that specialize in this area of work.

Wood items are usually simple to replicate, and if a wooden finish is intended, it may even be possible to find a piece of old timber that matches the original. Alternatively, wood can be aged and colored. Contact a local finish carpenter, wood turner or wood carver. Stone masons will also be able to carve replacement items, although for complicated shapes in stone it is often cheaper to make a mould from the original and then to cast a replacement using a mixture of stonedust and white cement, mixed to match the color.

RESTORING OLD FLOORS

Beneath the floor-covering of rooms or halls in older properties there is often a lovely wood, tiled or stone floor that only needs to be cleaned and finished to look like new.

Wood floors and stairs will usually require some sanding before they can be refinished. Mechanical sanders are available for rent in most towns and will take the work out of cleaning a large area; small hand-held electric models can be used for smaller or inaccessible areas.

Remember to remove any protruding nails or other obstacles that may damage the sander before starting work, and make sure that the area is well ventilated. Although very efficient, mechanical sanders do produce an enormous amount of dust, so it is sensible to cover or remove furniture, and to put heavy tape around any interior doors in order to prevent dust spreading all over the house. Since the dust is very unpleasant, it is wise to wear a mask; these are available from paint stores. Start with a coarse grade sandpaper to remove major marks and gradually work down to a fine grade.

A wide variety of finishes are available for wood floors, ranging from simple natural oils and waxes to hard-wearing polyurethane sealants. There are also a number of products available for coloring wood, either as separate dyes or as ready-colored oils, waxes and finishes. Wood parquet floors can be treated in the same way as wood boards. However, if the blocks have lifted or sunk, it may be necessary to remove them and then to relay a level substrate onto which the blocks can be positioned.

Stone flooring should not be sanded and may require a chemical cleaning agent. Expert advice should be sought, as stone is easily damaged and discolored when exposed, and can be very costly to replace.

Insulation

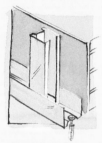

New homes are usually built with energy conservation in mind and so are well insulated. With alterations to older properties, this should be one of the first areas to attend to; the results should be improved comfort and lower heating bills. Improving insulation is also often part of major repairs.

EXCESSIVE INSULATION

Insulation is of benefit only if it is properly carried out. If not, it may even cause damage. Insulation does not mean closing off every chink and seam. Cooking and bathing put water vapor into the air and if it cannot escape, it will condense on the nearest part of the house that is cold. This is usually the window frames, glass of the windows, and the ground floor, which can be damaged by excessive moisture. Good ventilation is the principal remedy for condensation. This can be achieved by, for instance, having ventilation grills built into the window frames. Daily airing is essential for a home. Dry air can be heated more quickly than damp air.

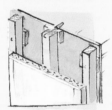

THE BEST INSULATION

The following points are worth noting:
■ Ensure that there is a small air cavity between the existing wall and the layer of insulation.
■ Fix a waterproof membrane between the insulation and the

Outside wall insulation seen from indoors, on wooden or steel frames.

> Glass with a high level of insulation is available; it is coated with a layer that prevents radiant heat from escaping. The space between the glazing units can also be filled with an inert gas, such as argon, which further limits the conduction of heat through the unit.

finishing layer of the wall (often sheetrock that is finished with plaster). For a partition wall made of either metal or timber studs, the insulation layer is fixed between the uprights. A waterproof layer is then fixed to the framework, followed by the sheetrock and its coat of plaster.

If there is a cavity wall, the house can be insulated by filling the cavity with a special insulation medium. Older houses rarely have cavity walls.

INSULATING FLOORS

A significant amount of heat is lost through the floor of a building, yet this is an area that people often forget to insulate. If the floor is of suspended construction, then there will be a space beneath the floor into which insulation can be installed. Where the flooring is laid directly on to a substrate, then a space for the insulation must be created below the floor. This can be done by removing and relaying the substrate, so as not to raise the finished floor level, which can prevent doors from opening. If raising the floor level is not a problem, then the flooring material can be removed and relaid onto battens, which lift the floor to create a space for the insulation.

INSULATING WITH GLASS

Double or even triple glazing can help save a considerable amount of energy. The insulation value of the different types varies. There are situations where double

glazing cannot be used: there may be too little depth to the window frames, or perhaps attractive antique leaded lights. In these cases secondary glazing can be used, installed on either the inside or outside of the property. Do not replace original windows simply in order to have double glazing, as you are likely to damage the character of the property. If you feel that double glazing is not suitable, then try adding extra insulation elsewhere, such as in the roof or under the floor, and fit a more efficient heating system. Before doing any of these, seal all the drafts.

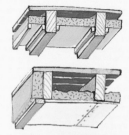

Four methods to insulate floors, depending upon the space beneath.

> ### WATERPROOFING LAYER
> It is important to place a layer that reduces moisture on the warm side (indoors) to prevent the insulation material from becoming wet, which would remove its insulating properties. Before treating the problem of moisture, try and treat the cause, which is usually poor ventilation.

METHODS OF INSULATING A ROOF

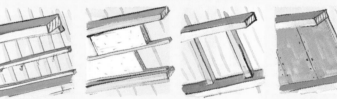

Retain character by placing insulation between the rafters, then covering it.

If you want the timber to be hidden, fix insulation panels to the rafters.

Poorly fitted windows and doors can cause horrible drafts that can make even a well-heated home uncomfortable. One option is to replace or repair the windows and doors or their frames, though it is usually possible to alleviate the problem by installing a weatherstrip. Several types are available, usually with a self-adhesive strip on one side and either a brush or other flexible material on the other. These can often be fitted on your own to the inside of the frame, and if there is sufficient space in the frame runner, these will be quite unobtrusive. You may need to call in a professional if hinges have to be moved.

Major repairs

During a structural survey, all the areas of a property that deteriorate and that are easily accessed will be carefully examined by a professional inspector. Such a survey is essential before buying any property, particularly if it is for rebuilding, remodelling or conversion to residential use. The findings will indicate the suitability of the building for its intended use to be assessed, along with the likely costs of building or repair work. This information can be used to negotiate a fair

THE STRUCTURAL SURVEY

During a structural house survey, each of the floors is assessed on many points – the baseboards, ridge tiles, window frames, hinges and locks, central heating, insulation and ventilation. The report indicates the condition of all these parts of the property, whether

repairs are needed immediately and what the eventual costs are likely to be.

GRANTS AND TAX BREAKS

Local and/or national governments may offer grants, tax breaks or other financial assistance for properties that are being

rebuilt, remodelled or converted. Contact local or regional building authorities for details of relevant programs.

TERMITES

During the structural survey, the property should be checked for termites. Holes in wood and wood dust on the floor are an indication of the presence of these pests. Wood wasps, fungi and lichen can also cause problems. If the structure has not been so badly damaged that replacement is needed, an exterminator can deal with the problem. Only have this work carried out after the timber in the house has been checked. If the problem is wet or dry rot or some other fungal infection, then your problem is likely to be poor ventilation. Solve this problem first (see

pages 162–3 for ideas) and then replace only those timbers that are structurally damaged.

MOISTURE IN THE HOME

Penetrating moisture is almost always due to bad pointing or masonry in the external walls. In such a case joints in the masonry have to be raked out and repointed after the walls have been cleaned. The masonry must be repaired or replaced. These measures are usually sufficient to solve the moisture problem. Rising moisture damages

the floor joists and other wooden construction, and efficient under-floor ventilation is essential to protect them.

Moisture can also damage the plaster on the inside walls. In this event, the walls will need to be impregnated to just beneath the floor joists to prevent the moisture from rising up the walls. It can also help if the metal flashing is replaced, particularly if a wall adjoins a balcony that does not drain well.

EXTERNAL TIMBER ROT

Neglected maintenance to gutter and paint and also inadequate under-floor ventilation can result in rotten timber.

To prevent this, the roofing and flashing must be replaced when they show signs of deterioration. The areas most prone to rot are those that suffer the greatest exposure to the elements, such as the soffits (under the eaves or roof overhang) and the fascia boards (the boards to which the rainwater system is attached). Regular maintenance and painting will restrict damage to these areas.

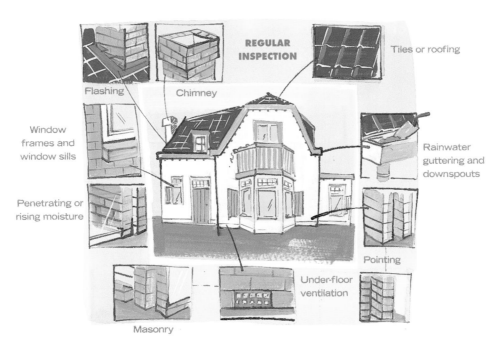

REGULAR INSPECTION

Tiles or roofing

Flashing

Chimney

Window frames and window sills

Rainwater guttering and downspouts

Penetrating or rising moisture

Pointing

Under-floor ventilation

Masonry

REPAIRING WINDOW FRAMES

Rotten window frames can be repaired if the damage is caught in the early stages. If detected early enough, it is sufficient to insert a special capsule that guards against dry rot. If the damage is a little more extensive, you will need to replace the damaged area back to good wood and treat the gap with special dry rot compound. After the frame has been filled, planed, sanded and painted, nothing should be seen of the repair. If the rot is more extensive, you can limit the cost and retain the original window by removing and replacing just the sill and a small part of the stile (the most vulnerable areas).

ORIGINAL GUTTERS

Plastic guttering and downspouts can be replaced with iron, zinc or even copper pipes that are cast or extruded to original patterns. The funnels at the top of the downspouts are also still available just as they used to be. Zinc and copper are expensive, but the range in terms of size and dimension is greater, and the life is longer, provided that they are well maintained. Metal will last for decades, provided they are painted regularly. Maintenance-free PVC versions are available from various manufacturers in many period patterns and styles.

Lighting

As well as having an important practical function, lighting has an enormous influence on the style and character of each room of the home. Successful lighting needs to be planned at a very early stage in the design process, before the wiring has been installed (see the section on wiring on page 162). Do not forget to plan exterior lighting around the home and garden, too. This is important for safety and security, as well as making an attractive feature.

MAKE A LIST

The best electrical fittings do not get noticed. If planned right, the lighting will not have any exposed wiring. The best time to rewire is while remodeling work is taking place. By making a check list for the alterations, you can prevent things having to be added or adapted later which could spoil your decorating. You may find it useful to make a scale plan of the room and draw out a wiring design. If you have already drawn up a plan to help you position your furniture, then you can add to this, placing light switches and sockets wherever they are required. Don't forget to add telephone and cable outlets, or sockets for table lamps, the stereo, television and VCR. This is also the time to arrange to lay speaker cables out of sight. If you have furniture in the center of a room and require a light, do not be afraid to place a electrical outlet in the floor, with a lid to conceal it when it is not in use. If you are rewiring, consider the position of the lighting; you do not just have to have a central pendant light. Consider spotlights, wall and table lights. You may choose to run more than one circuit, perhaps having a separate lighting circuit for ceiling, wall and table lights.

SPECIAL WISHES

On the final check list you can add the things you missed before: an additional light switch on the other side of the room; a telephone outlet or extra circuit in the kitchen; and an electrical outlet in the center of the room, under the sofa or coffee table, for instance, for a standard lamp. Bear in mind the demands of modern equipment: where previously only a refrigerator and washing machine drew current, many homes now also have a microwave, a computer, a dryer, freezer and dishwasher, all demanding energy. Once you have a plan that works for you, you can use this as the basis for obtaining estimates from some electricians. Ask for estimates from several firms because prices can vary widely.

STANDARD RULES FOR POWER OUTLETS

In principle, two power outlets are needed in each room or area of the home. Whenever the distance between outlets is greater than 12 feet (3.5m), fix another double outlet between them just in case.

THE HEIGHT OF THE POWER OUTLETS

The power outlets in the corners of the room can be placed as low as possible so as to be unobtrusive. Sometimes the local energy company stipulates a minimum height. There are many variables and specific regulations, so before you start your alterations, check with your electric company what the rules are for your locality. For table lights, kitchen or computer equipment, it may be useful to place the power outlets at waist height. For handicapped access you may also find waist-height sockets more easily accessible.

CABLES OUT OF SIGHT

A power outlet in the floor with a metal lid can be an ideal solution for avoiding trailing wires. This floor outlet is mounted in a metal housing and can be fixed to either wooden or concrete floors. Try to decide where the sofa or coffee table will be when carrying out alterations since this is often the most suitable place for a power outlet.

DIMMERS: LESS LIGHT, MORE ATMOSPHERE

Lower wattage lamps give a warmer light, but sometimes plenty of light is needed. A dimmer switch makes both possible. Nowadays many light fittings and lamps are sold with dimmers fitted to their leads. If not, this is easily done by replacing the existing switch with a dimmer. Standard dimmer switches cannot be used with halogen lamps that work with a transformer to lower the voltage; for instance, 12 volt halogen spotlights need a special dimmer. Halogen lamps that work at regular voltage and normal incandescent bulbs can, however, be controlled by the same standard dimmer. Energy saving lamps cannot be used with dimmers.

BASIC LIGHTING

Basic lighting does not have to mean a pendant light fixed in the center of the ceiling. The main light switch can also control lighting for the dining table and various table or standard lamps. This creates a more intimate atmosphere when you turn on the lights.

LIGHTING WITH TWO FUNCTIONS

By fixing a dimmer to both the main and mood lighting, these lights can be used for both main illumination and mood setting. Uplighting – standard lamps directed towards the ceiling – light the ceiling more strongly, which gives an impression that it is higher.

FEATURE LIGHTING

For the lighting of paintings or prints, for instance, feature lighting can be used. This can be done with spotlights recessed into the ceiling, surface mounted or mounted on track, or with a low-voltage cable system.

To avoid pictures acting as mirrors and to avoid

shadows, feature lighting should be placed on the ceiling 32 to 48 inches (80 to 120 cm) away from the wall. The higher the ceiling, the further from the wall the lights need to be fitted. Built-in spotlights, especially halogen, can be fitted only in lowered false ceilings. Be aware of potential fire hazards, since halogen lamps give off lots of heat.

SEEING THE LIGHT

Do not be embarrassed to ask different lighting companies to visit you at home in the evening with samples of their lighting so that you can select what is best for your interior.

WARM LIGHT

Fluorescent tubes provide well-diffused light and are now available in a range of pastel shades such as pale yellow, light green or apricot. These can produce a very soft, warm light.

LOW-PROFILE SPOTS

Low-profile spotlights are available for building into the bottom of wall units or shelves above the kitchen counters without taking up any cupboard space.

The bathroom

If you are rebuilding, remodeling, converting or building anew, then you will be able to design your bathroom with a clean sheet of paper. On your scale floor plan you will be able to try out several different combinations of fixtures in the same way as you did with your furniture. You can draw your fixtures as they would look from above, cut these out and then move them around your plan. Scale drawings of many models are now available in manufacturers' brochures. If you have the space, you can create an elegant bathroom designed for relaxation; but even a small bathroom has enormous potential with the right choice of bath and toilet fixtures.

CHOOSING SLIMLINE FIXTURES

Before talking to the builder or plumber, draw up a list of the bath fixtures that will be needed.

If there is not room for a bidet, separate shower, bath, double wash pedestals and a toilet, there are other convenient solutions. Baths combined with showers have good flat areas for showering, and there is a wide range of decorative shower panels and curtains from which to choose. There are also baths specially designed for smaller spaces. Instead of twin pedestals, two small basins that are sufficient for washing and shaving can be fitted in a counter. The toilet for the bathroom or half-bath is increasingly

available in a wide range of models. For a toilet that can be fitted at the height you prefer, there are suspended or wall-mounted models. These make it easier to clean the floor surrounding the toilet and also to keep the space looking far less cluttered.

If space is very restricted, then a wet bathroom, where the room itself forms the shower enclosure, is the ideal solution. The walls and floor of such a bathroom are usually tiled and the floor slopes from the walls so that water drains into a central drain.

A small downstairs half-bathroom is a popular feature in many homes. The space under the stairs or an old closet may be the ideal location for this.

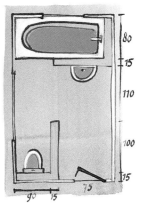

Partition walls permit separate toilet and shower corners.

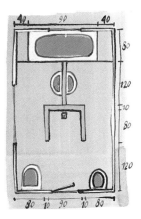

A central wall makes a shower and two washbasins possible.

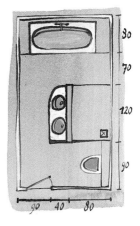

Plate glass and a partition wall form a shower area.

Annotated measurements are in centimeters: 90cm = 3ft

When adding a new bathroom, be certain that there is sufficient space for the necessary plumbing required by code.

COLORED GLASS BUILDING BLOCKS

The layout of the bathroom can be made very interesting by the use of plain or colored glass building blocks. They let light in for a spacious feeling and are available in a variety of finishes.

PARTITION WALLS

Bathroom fixtures can be placed anywhere in the bathroom, even in the middle of the room, since free-standing partition walls can be constructed. Partition walls do not have to reach the ceiling: a height of just 4 feet (120 cm) means that wash-basins can be hidden without making the space seem smaller. Additionally, the top of the wall can be used as a shelf or as the base for a free-standing mirror. A partition wall need not only be functional: it can also have an effect on the decorative scheme of the bathroom. Take the top of the partition wall as the top line for the tiling to create a natural panelling.

This can be featured by using a line of different colored border tiles.

TOILET: PLACE IT ANYWHERE

Partition walls make it possible for wiring and plumbing to be hidden from view, as the necessary ducts can be concealed in the wall space. The toilet can therefore be positioned wherever you want in the bathroom. Greater flexibility is offered by combination toilets that incorporate a pump to remove the waste. With these, the toilet can be placed some distance away from the sewage pipe, or even in a basement.

WINDOW BLINDS FOR THE BATHROOM

The best blinds for the bathroom let light in by day and give privacy at night. They must be capable of withstanding excessive moisture yet also be stylish. Stainless steel louvre blinds meet these criteria. There are also various fabrics that are suitable for the bathroom.

They can be used for both roller blinds and curtains. Make sure that the curtain rail or mounting system is moisture-resistant. The disadvantage of curtains is that they let in almost no light. Wooden blinds are also available in a water-resistant version. Louvred shutters that fit to the inside of a window frame are another choice. Some types are adjustable to control the amount of light that is let in.

SAFETY IN THE BATHROOM

Anti-slip tiles are particularly important in the bathroom, especially if there are children or elderly people in the household. These are available in many colors and designs. There are even tiles designed specially for the 'children's bathroom'. If these are used together with a thermostatic shower control, then children can safely learn to take their first showers unaided, and elderly people can retain their independence longer.

Consider, too, special corner mouldings that can be used to round off corners such as by the shower partition, so that no one risks cutting or bruising themselves. They are a delightful change from squared-off tiles.

LARGER THAN USUAL SHOWER-HEAD

Large shower-heads are currently very popular, as are special multi-function showers with multiple sprays and/or feature settings, like massage or steam. Such showers need to have a hot water system capable of delivering at least 3$\frac{1}{2}$ gallons (16 l) per minute. Once mixed with cold, that equals a fairly massive 5$\frac{1}{2}$ gallons (25 l) of warm water per minute. By comparison, a normal shower uses 1$\frac{3}{4}$–3$\frac{1}{4}$ gallons per minute (8–15 l). The same requirement applies if there are side sprays in addition to the main shower-head. A hot water heater with a minimum capacity of 33 gallons (150 l) is needed for these more complex showers.

THERMOSTATIC CONTROL

Because the thermostatic valve, once properly adjusted, automatically mixes water to the right temperature, it is both easy and safe for children to shower on their own. This is particularly useful in stopping a sudden blast of cold water when hot water is drawn somewhere else in the home.

THE FLOOR

Tiles and terrazzo have long been considered excellent bathroom materials for the floor, walls or vanity unit. They are particularly convenient for a wet bathroom (see page 167) because a drain can be included in such floors. With these materials, the bathroom and shower area can be seamlessly joined, with the shower floor slightly

lower so that it can be quickly dried with a sponge mop. The lack of edges and seams makes it easier to keep clean. Terrazzo comes in almost every color and a range of finishes. It is laid and then polished in place. Seamless bathrooms are also achievable with terrazzo, using smooth edging strips. Wooden and laminate flooring is also now available for use in bathrooms, as are some types of stone and marble. Vinyl floors are popular and easy to keep clean. Finally, a cork-tiled floor can be made completely waterproof and will provide a warm and easily maintained floor covering.

A PLACE FOR THE WASHING MACHINE AND DRYER

The washing machine and dryer are often located in the kitchen, or a separate wash or utility room, positioned close to where washing can be hung out to dry. However, some owners prefer to install their washing machine and dryer upstairs near the bedrooms, where most of the dirty laundry is generated. If the location is to be the bathroom, then the wiring for appliances has to be approved by an electrician in order to meet the strict safety requirements. See the illustration above and page 162 for information on installation.

HEATING IN THE BATHROOM

The central heating system can be used to supply under-floor heating for the bathroom as well as radiators and perhaps a heated towel rack. Under-floor heating is an ideal heat source for the bathroom. If you are not installing under-floor heating throughout the house, there are systems that can be added to a single room that hardly raise the floor level. Electrical heating or small-bore tubing can be laid under the floor. Another new alternative is mirror heating (not to be confused with mirrors that have a de-misting element fitted behind them). If the mirror is large enough (the installer can calculate this), the system can heat the entire bathroom. If the mirror is not large enough, a small decorative radiator or towel rack can be used as additional heating. If the bathroom has under-floor heating, a towel rack or radiator can still be run from the hot water supply, if it is a pumped system.

SMALL BATHROOM, SPACIOUS LAYOUT

If space is at a premium, then one way of making a bathroom seem larger is to place two washbasins with their backs to each other, each facing a partition wall about 67 inches (170cm) high (see illustration). This makes the bathroom seem wider than if the basins were placed next to each other.
Other ways of creating an impression of space include carefully located mirrors, good lighting and light colored walls.

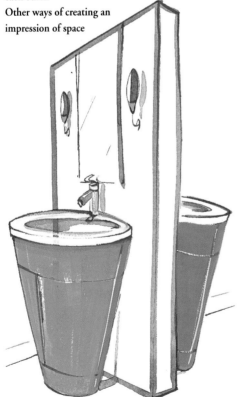

VENTILATION

All 'wet' areas such as bathrooms need to be ventilated to prevent the build up of damp, stale air. Bathroom ventilation was traditionally provided by vents or open windows, but this has been replaced in modern homes by mechanical ventilation. Motorized fans located in an outside wall or window extract stale air, and fresh air is drawn in via vents. Bathrooms located away from external walls, for instance under the stairs, can be fittted with a duct to a remotely located extractor fan.

The kitchen

During the building or renovation of a kitchen it is often necessary to consider a wide range of issues. How often do you eat at home? How much space is needed for cooking? Does the whole family eat together? Do you want to be able to eat in the kitchen? Do you need wall cabinets or is there enough storage space in the base units? From the following information you can create a check list of all your needs.

CONSIDER THE LOCATION

When you have bought a new home or are intending to carry out extensive renovations, it seems obvious to leave the kitchen where it is because all the plumbing and wiring is there, and there are usually fitted units that might not take kindly to being ripped out of one room and reinstalled in another. However, if there are good reasons for wanting to move the kitchen from the back of the house to the front (often to achieve more and better light or to move to a larger room), it is possible, because the main gas, water and electrical connections are usually extendable. Where you have an attractive rear garden there is a distinct advantage in such a move. The living room can be opened up across the entire width of the back of the house, and the addition of patio doors opening onto the garden means that the garden can become part of the newly enlarged living room.

KEEP IT PRACTICAL

Before deciding on a kitchen it is important to think about how you use it. Do you mainly cook quick meals for two? If so, then a stove top with four burners or rings and a microwave oven will do. If you like to cook in advance for the entire week, or regularly cook extensive dinners, think in terms of a six-burner range, or one with variable rings that will take larger pans. You will also need a separate oven or one combined with a microwave. Having assessed your culinary lifestyle, make sure that there is room for a freezer of suitable capacity. The size of the kitchen has a bearing on the types of cabinets you should choose. Narrower kitchens are better with double

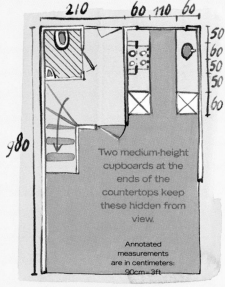

210 60 110 60
50
60
50
50
60
980

Two medium-height cupboards at the ends of the countertops keep these hidden from view.

Annotated measurements are in centimeters: 90cm = 3ft

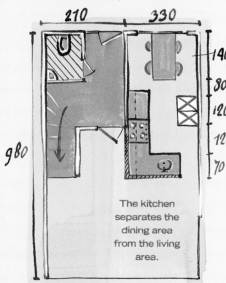

210 330
140
80
120
120
70
980

The kitchen separates the dining area from the living area.

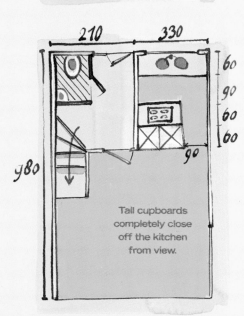

210 330
60
90
60
60
980
90

Tall cupboards completely close off the kitchen from view.

cabinet doors with a smaller opening radius of just 1 foot (30 cm). Finally, the refrigerator and freezer, stove top and sink must be within easy reach of each other, without any obstructions. Draw a plan of your ideas in order to visualize your kitchen, and try to imagine how it will look in three dimensions. The plan can bring to light various matters that need to be borne in mind.

On which side of the refrigerator should the door open? How much room will there be to move around between the counter and the kitchen appliances if they are installed as on the plan? An efficient kitchen is one where the cook can perform all the necessary tasks with a minimum of movement. So having the dishwasher near the dish cabinet and cutlery drawer will mean speedy unloading, and storing frequently used cooking ingredients near to the main worktop will avoid unnecessary trips back and forth.

EXTRA SPACE

If you are remodeling, converting or building your own home, consider devoting some space to a separate utility room or even a walk-in pantry. A utility room is the ideal spot for locating a deep-freeze, the washer/dryer, extra storage and even the pet's bed.

POWER AND LIGHT

Following the instructions for drawing up a plan on page 162, you can make a plan of the new kitchen's electrical requirements. Firstly, there must be sufficient outlets for small appliances and proper outlets for major appliances. Four outlets in the wall is not extravagant luxury. They can also be positioned in the bottom of the wall units. Remember that the washing machine should ideally be on a separate circuit and placed on a level floor. This might mean strengthening part of a wooden floor close to the outlet for the washing machine.

A golden rule for the kitchen is that nothing should block the path between the lighting and the work surface. The lighting therefore needs to be fixed as close to the work surface as possible. If there are no wall units, a cable can be installed above the counter for halogen spotlights which give directable light. Spots with clamps that can be attached to shelves are a good alternative. Small fluorescent tubes were once widely used under wall units but there are now more attractive options. Halogen lights on a rail are very convenient because they can be moved at will. There are also extremely low-profile halogen spotlights that can be built into the underside of wall units.

WALL UNITS OR NOT?

A kitchen always seems bigger if there are no wall cabinets but not everyone has sufficient storage space without hanging units on the wall. If you need them but want to keep a sense of spaciousness, choose wall units with glass doors or with open shelves or racks. A stainless steel rod or rack on which you can hang meat cleavers, whisks and small pans is an attractive addition. Cupboards beneath the work surface can be more effectively used with slide-out racks or plenty of drawers, and turntables

for the corner units. Drawers can also be fitted at the base of the cupboards, if it is made higher than usual.

CHANGING THE COLOR OF YOUR KITCHEN

Do you want to change the color of the cabinet doors in your kitchen? If so, then there are several possibilities to consider:

■ If the doors and drawer fronts are of wood, clean them well, sand them and paint them. Add two coats of varnish for protection against chipping and staining.

■ Plastic-coated cabinet doors can be rubbed down with fine sandpaper or steel wool after they have been thoroughly cleaned. Coat them with an oil-based primer which provides a base for paint, then apply the paint of your choice – either oil- or water-based – on top. For a finer finish, try your hand at some dragging or stippling, or opt for the fashionable distressed look by applying two coats of

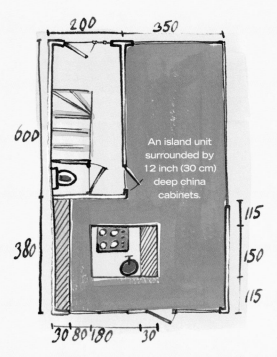

An island unit surrounded by 12 inch (30 cm) deep china cabinets.

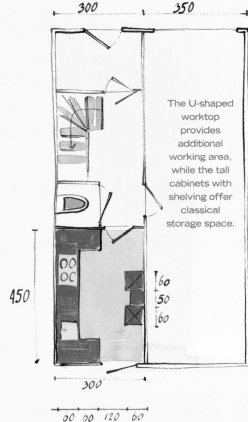

The U-shaped worktop provides additional working area, while the tall cabinets with shelving offer classical storage space.

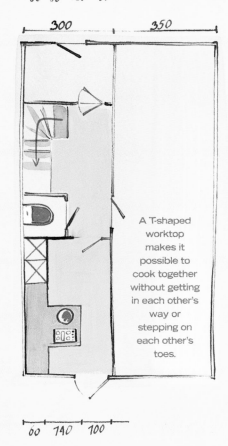

A T-shaped worktop makes it possible to cook together without getting in each other's way or stepping on each other's toes.

paint and rubbing the top one away in places to reveal the underlying color. Another idea is to use a fairly new product that produces a wood grain effect on non-wood surfaces. Once you have finished, either cover the decorated cupboard doors with two coats of varnish or take the doors to a paint shop that can coat them at the right temperature and pressure with hardened lacquer, protecting them against scratches and other marks.

■ Another possibility is to cover the doors with toughened plastic sheeting in a new color. Get it done by a carpenter or furniture maker, because this is precision work. The cupboard hinges will need to be adjustable because the fronts will now be slightly thicker.

■ A metal worker or furniture maker can also cover them with stainless steel or zinc sheet for a thoroughly professional-looking kitchen.

WIDE RANGE OF COUNTERTOP MATERIALS

The choice of work surface will depend on its appearance, wear-resistance and, of course, the cost. Materials for work surfaces are available to suit every taste, but some are more easily damaged than others. Here is an overview of the main choices.

■ A terrazzo or granolithic finish is classical. The fragments of marble or granite can be given any color. It is very hard wearing.

■ Wood is available with varnished or oiled finishes, but it needs regular

maintenance because any damage to the surface coating will make the wood porous. Laminate wood – a less expensive but more hard-wearing alternative to solid wood – is worth considering.

■ Artificial stone is a new material for the kitchen. Available in various designs and colors, it is heat resistant and does not crack.

■ Granite is suitable because of its hardness. It has beautiful natural figuring and color. The surface withstands cracking and heat, but dark colored substances can stain it.

■ Plastic laminate counter- tops are available in a wide choice of designs and colors. Chemicals and acids do not damage them, but they are usually not completely heat resistant.

WALL BEHIND THE COUNTERTOP

New ideas for replacing tiles are constantly appearing on the market. A stainless steel panel to give an attractive and professional look to the kitchen, or plastic sheet glued to a board and then fixed to the wall are just two examples. Further ideas include a sheet of fiberglass or a plaster wall that has been decorated and then coated with a water-based varnish.

KITCHEN FLOORS

The choice for kitchen flooring is as broad as the

choice for countertops.

■ Linoleum offers a wide range of designs and colors. It needs a well-levelled base and for best results should be laid by a professional.

■ Stone slabs are dirt resistant because of their hard surface and also wear resistant. Stone is a timeless material that will last and last, but it needs to be laid on a solid floor base. Stone slabs can be either smooth, for a formal look, or uneven for a more rustic look.

■ Quarry tiles can be laid in attractive patterns. Their disadvantage is that they are porous and so are prone to staining unless waxed or treated regularly to keep them dirt resistant.

■ Laminated panels are available in various designs and colors. The better quality ones are suitable for the kitchen.

■ Wood or parquet creates a warm feeling but does not score so well in terms of resistance to water and dirt.

■ Marble and stone have a very long life, though marble needs a protective finish to avoid being stained.

■ Tiles are wear resistant and easy to keep clean. These hard flooring solutions such as stone and tiles are perfect for use with under-floor heating, which is the ideal heat source for a kitchen as it is both comfortable and unobtrusive.

Color and paint

The easiest way to change the style of a home is to paint it. How you can achieve professional looking paintwork is covered here in this mini-course on painting.

EACH SPACE ITS OWN COLOR

Most important when choosing colors is your personal preference. But the dimensions of the room can also be an important consideration. The basic principal of using color is that darker colors make a space or an object look smaller, while lighter hues have the opposite effect. Rooms facing north that never get any sun receive cool light. This can be countered by using warmer colors such as red, yellow, orange or shades of brown. Those that face south get plenty of sunlight and benefit from softer shades that reflect less than white. Blue and green tints are not too cool to use in these circumstances and therefore work well.

CHOOSING COLORS: PLAYING WITH EFFECTS

It is quite astonishing how different a room can look with the careful use of color. The apparent width, height or length of a room can be influenced by it. A darker ceiling makes the room seem lower. If you need to increase the impression of height in a room, then the answer is to paint the ceiling lighter than the walls. Vertical stripes also create a sense of height. These can be in either contrasting colors or more muted stripes. The width of a room can be made to seem wider by using horizontal stripes. Finally, a large room can be made more intimate by painting the walls a darker color.

If you want color but also the tranquillity of white, you can paint a 'panel' of color or colorwash up to about 3 feet (90 cm) high, perhaps with a border, leaving the wall above this white. For a really restful room, paint the baseboard the same color as the lower part of the wall.

MINI-COURSE ON PAINTING

Once the colors have been chosen, the rest is down to your painting skills. Here are some tips.

1 ASSESSING WHAT NEEDS TO BE DONE

Whether the existing paint needs to be stripped completely depends upon its condition. Paintwork that is not more than two years old with little damage requires only sanding and cleaning. If there are cracks or blisters, you can check with a piece of adhesive tape how well the paint is adhering to the surface. Stick the tape on a weak patch and then remove it. If paint is left sticking to the tape, then the paint in that place needs to be stripped off. If more than 25 per cent is bad, it would be sensible to remove it all.

2 GOOD TOOLS ARE HALF THE ANSWER

Old paint is removed using a sharp paint scraper or a filling or stripping knife. Make sure that the blade is smooth, because a rough blade might easily damage the surface of the wood. Besides the well-known triangular scraper for large surfaces, there are also various smaller scrapers for dealing with wooden mouldings (though anything delicate should be sanded instead). Burning off the paint can damage the wood and should never be done indoors. Much better is a heat gun which softens the paint, making it easier to remove. Paint strippers work efficiently but have the disadvantage that the wood has to be thoroughly cleaned and rinsed off afterwards. Strippers are quite corrosive and give off vapors that can be harmful if inhaled. It is best to avoid using them in poorly ventilated spaces or where there may be children present.

3 KNOTS CAUSE WEAK SPOTS

Paint does not adhere very well to knots or resinous wood. They are best dealt with by drilling them out or removing with a chisel. Knots from which resin weeps can sometimes be closed by heating them with a propane torch. Fill the holes with filler and, when dry, sand down to a level surface. Alternatively, knots can be sealed to prevent resin from bleeding from them and blistering the paintwork.

4 PREPARING FOR PAINTING

After the old paint has been removed, the condition of the wood can be assessed. If rot is discovered, small areas can be restored. Cut back the affected wood to sound timber and treat with wood preservative. Fill with a special filler. For larger areas, use a piece of plexiglass to stop the filler from falling out before it has hardened. Place plastic film between the plexiglass and filler so that it can be removed easily when the filler is dry.

5 PROTECTING AGAINST ROT

The bottom corners of window and door frames are the most susceptible to rotting. Water becomes trapped in the cracks left when wood dries out. Clean them out to enlarge them and fill with a compound that remains elastic, such as a mastic sealer, and which can be painted over. Splits in window sills can be treated in the same way. Broken putty or window compound also lets in water. Replace the putty with glazing beads. Soften the existing putty with a heat gun to make it easier to remove. Smear a butyl glazing compound around the edge and push the beading into position. Fix it in place with small brads. Remove any excess compound. Cracked putty indoors can be handled in the same way.

6 RECOATING WOOD STAIN, EMULSION AND WHITEWASH

Wood stain only needs any loose flakes to be scraped off before it is re-applied. Sanding and cleaning is quite adequate.

 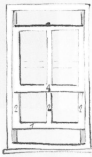 

The numbering on the different types of window shows the ideal sequence in which to paint them. Make sure with sash windows that the sash cord does not get painted.

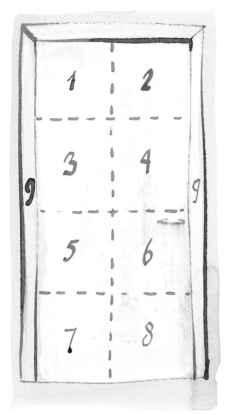 

If you follow the numbered sequence shown for painting doors, you will achieve an attractive, even finish. This is particularly important with gloss paint. Laying off or brushing out the paint must be done, as far as possible, in only one direction.

Emulsion on walls and ceilings simply requires any cracks to be repaired before being wiped down with water to which a little ammonia has been added. It can then be re-painted. In older houses there may still be a layer of whitewash (a lime-based substance used for whitening walls, also known as distemper) on ceilings and walls. This cannot just be painted over because emulsion paint reacts with the lime in the whitewash, causing it to bubble and crack. Remove such a layer with a wet sponge and a filling knife or with wallpaper paste, which you paint on as thickly as possible and then brush off when it is almost dry. This is a convenient way to deal with mouldings and other ornamentation. If there appears to be remaining whitewash on a ceiling that you have just painted with emulsion, remove the patches, fill and then repaint them.

7 BEFORE YOU START PAINTING WOODWORK

Once the old or poor quality layers of paint have been removed, it is time to start rubbing down the woodwork. Use a fairly fine grade sandpaper for this to achieve a smooth surface. An electric sander gives the best results for relatively large, smooth areas, but always sand mouldings and beadings by hand or you might damage either the window pane or the moulding. Pine and teak both contain oily substances to which paint does not adhere easily, so these sorts of woods need to be thoroughly cleaned with ammonia or thinners before paint is applied.

8 PRIMING: THE FIRST LAYER

Bare wood that is to be painted must be primed first so that the top coats will bond.

Where the wood is to be painted a dark color, use a dark primer. The primer makes the wood fibers

stand up so that the surface is made slightly rough. A light 'stroking' with sandpaper is sufficient to smooth this down and to help the next coat to hold. Always clean after sanding.

If you are painting wooden parts that are held together by tongue and groove, such as weather boarding or flooring on a veranda, it is best to prime the tongue and groove before assembling them because this protects them better against water. Any unevenness can then be made good with filler – indoors with special paint-like filler or quick filler (although this often cracks) and outdoors with liquid wood. Once this is dry, sand again with very fine grade paper. Clean the timber before painting so that it is smooth and free of grease. Wood stain does not need an undercoat, so the first layer is the stain itself.

9 CONDITIONS FOR THE FINAL COAT

When you apply the top coats the weather should be dry but not too warm. Never paint in full sun. Indoors make sure that everything that you paint is free from dust and

grease. The first layer of the final coat never covers immediately. To prevent runs, apply two or more thin coats. Try to brush out (or lay) the paint in one direction, especially with gloss paint. If using a roller, run a brush just once lightly over the recently painted section to prevent air bubbles. Rub down lightly between each coat of paint and then clean and degrease before the next coat with water or ammonia. Finally, give horizontal parts of window frames a final coat. Wood stain always needs three coats for good cover. Paints are now available that include both primer and top coat in one, making painting woodwork faster and easier. These are available in matte, silk and gloss finishes. For a smooth, drip-free finish, these paints are still best applied in two or three thin coats.

MAINTAINING NEW PAINT

It is important to clean painted surfaces regularly because this keeps the paint in better condition, reducing the frequency of repainting. Inspect paintwork every year for cracking, paying special attention to horizontal areas and the parts adjoining them. Gloss paint needs repainting about every six years; opaque stain about every four years, and transparent stain about every three years.

PAINTING METAL PARTS

Before painting pipes, radiators or metal staircase rails you must remove any rust. With new iron and steel, the blue/black layer needs to be removed because this prevents the paint from adhering well. Surface rust is removed with a steel brush; deeper rust requires special sandpaper or a sanding disk. After degreasing, give two coats of metal primer followed by two coats of paint.

Flooring

The choice of floor covering has a tremendous impact on the style of a room, not only aesthetically in terms of its color, pattern and surface texture, but also practically in terms of comfort and its feel underfoot. Whether you choose a soft or hard floor covering depends upon the use of the room, the floor base and the position of the room in the home. Here is an overview of some of the options and the factors that might influence your selection.

TILES, TERRAZZO AND CEMENT FLOORS

A stone-type floor such as tiles, terrazzo or a fine-finish cement floor places an additional load on the floor which has to be considered. If the load is too great, the pressure on the sleeper walls may be too severe, causing cracking. The company supplying the flooring material can provide extensive information about the requirements for the floor base.

A stone floor is ideal for use with an under-floor heating system, which is both energy efficient and a very comfortable method of heating.

If you choose terrazzo or cement flooring that is to be coated, the floor needs to have an expansion joint – a small break that is filled with either plastic, aluminium, or a brass strip. This is necessary to permit the floor to expand when warm. Similar measures are also necessary for tiled floors, but the joints between tiles provide the solution.

In areas of less than 13 × 13 feet (4 × 4 m) this is not necessary. If you do not want a difference in levels and also wish to avoid over-stressing the construction of the floor, tiles can be laid on the floor base. If you have a

level concrete floor, tiles can be adhered directly to it with excellent results.

LAYING ONTO WOOD

If you have a wood rather than a cement floor, you can successfully lay tiles on this too. Level the boards by screwing ¾ inch (18 mm) thick marine plywood to the base, preferably diagonally to the floor boards. Flat tiles can then easily be fixed to this surface.

FITTED CARPETS

The recent development of computer-controlled cutting techniques has significantly increased the ability to lay diverse patterns in carpet. By using two different colors of carpet, a neat stair runner can easily be created. For living rooms, a contrasting border is possible, or two different colors can be divided by a curved line

The advantage of carpet is that it diffuses light in a pleasing way, which is particularly useful for south-facing rooms. If you want to furnish your home with as little furniture as possible perhaps with high ceilings, fitted carpet can solve the problem of resounding noise.

QUALITY INFORMATION

Carpets have precise details about their suitability for different types of use clearly indicated in a standard quality system. The information on the back of the carpet helps you to choose the right carpet and indicates, for instance, if it is anti-static, and whether it is suitable for stairs or other main circulation areas, or only for use in bedrooms.

LAYING CARPET

The backing of the carpet determines how it is to be laid. There are textile-, foam- and latex-backed carpets. Only foam-

backed carpet can be laid without underlay directly on the floor with adhesive – although first laying hardboard is often advisable. In rooms up to about 19 square yards (16 m²), carpet can be loose laid. In this case it is sufficient to adhere the edges using double-sided carpet tape. If the backing is of textile or latex, an underlay is necessary. Normally such carpets are laid with tackless edging strips. When textile- or latex-backed carpets are laid without padding they are likely to wear badly. Without springy padding, they are also less comfortable to walk on.

Padding should not be used with under-floor heating. The carpet must be stuck directly to the floor, which slightly reduces the efficiency of the heating.

THE PILE

Carpet comes in a wide assortment of types and lengths of pile. Whether the pile is open or closed depends upon how the knots are looped. If these are cut through, the pile sticks up to create open pile. Where the loops are not cut, they give the carpet a curly (or bouclé)

finish. The number of loops and the way they are attached to the backing determine the quality and price of the carpet.

VELVET EFFECT

Many open-pile carpets, such as velors, exhibit what is known as 'shading' – depending upon the direction of the pile, light is either reflected or absorbed, making the carpet seem darker or lighter, just like velvet. This is particularly noticeable after any vacuuming. If you wish to avoid this, examine carpet in a showroom from different angles and run your hand over the pile to judge the effect. Another way to avoid this phenomenon is to choose closed-looped carpets.

NATURAL FLOOR COVERINGS

Floor coverings made from natural fibers such as coir (coconut husk),

seagrass, sisal and jute are becoming increasingly popular, as their neutral shades work well with many styles of interior decor. The natural fibers are woven into coarse, hardwearing floor coverings in a variety of textured patterns. Most natural floor coverings are latex backed and so need to be used in conjunction with padding. Fitting techniques are the same with carpet and other soft floor coverings.

LAYING CARPET YOURSELF

Before laying carpet, the floor must be dry, level, firm and smooth. With wood floors, that usually means laying plywood or chipboard. Any gaps or cracks in a concrete floor must be filled before the carpet is laid.

Carpet is usually laid with adhesive or stretched (work for a craftsman). Special environmentally friendly adhesives without solvents are available for gluing carpets.

Where carpet meets other floor coverings it should be terminated with a strip that looks neat and protects it from wear. Two different carpets are joined with a tackless edging strip. These are strips with hooks that are fixed to the floor to hold the carpet. Special edge strips are used to finish the carpet off neatly where it borders a smooth floor such as wood.

LOOKING AFTER CARPET

For stains use clean lukewarm water with a few drops of liquid detergent. Carbonated water is a good alternative – the bubbles work in the same way as the liquid detergent. Stain removers or commercial carpet cleaners can also be used, but do not use too much. Work from the edge to the middle of the stain, dabbing, not rubbing, then rinse with a little water. Stains in sisal floor-covering can be removed with a brush and luke-warm water with a little ammonia. Chewing gum is removed from carpet and sisal by first cooling it with ice cubes.

VINYL FLOOR COVERING

Vinyl-covered floors are easy to keep clean and can be very inexpensive. For vinyl to stay nice looking though it needs a completely smooth base. Laying vinyl yourself is relatively easy but preparing the right base is far more trouble and usually demands a craftsman's skills. If laying vinyl yourself, work from the center of the room. Lay the surplus up over the baseboard and smooth the vinyl out towards the edges. Fold the excess back double against the baseboard and cut with a sharp craft knife. Cut slightly above the fold for the right size. If you cut on the fold line the vinyl will be slightly too short. Practice with an off-cut so that you can get used to where to cut. If the vinyl bubbles up, you have not cut off enough. Lay a ruler along the baseboard and cut a small additional amount off. A couple of inches is usually more than enough.

LINOLEUM AND SIMILAR FLOORING

The laying of linoleum and other similar flooring material is work for a specialist. The substrate must be completely level and smooth before laying. Solid floors are levelled using a liquid levelling compound. Wood floors are prepared with a rigid board or sheet material of ¾ to ⅞ inch (18 to 22 mm) thickness. Beautiful patterns can be formed with linoleum, using repeating patterns, edge designs, wavy borders, and even totally contrasting colors. When this type of flooring is laid in damp rooms, it is important that the seams are welded. When the floor has been laid, it is coated with a protective layer, because linoleum is not water-resistant. A water-resistant treatment should be applied twice a year. Cleaning is quite easy – vacuum and mop with a well-wrung mop, using water with a little floor cleaner added.

LAMINATED FLOOR

Laminated floor is a relatively new type of flooring. Its great advantages are that it is an extremely convenient flooring, which is easy to lay yourself, can be much cheaper than solid wood floors, is colorfast and its top layer is extremely tough and wear resistant (unlike the varnish layer of parquet). It is made of laminations of different materials: a waterproof layer, a thin board, a thin layer with a photographic print of wood grain and finally an extremely hard clear plastic layer. Laminated flooring is available in various sizes, depending upon the manufacturing process, (8 × 8 in, 8 × 24 in and 8 × 48 in / 20 × 20 cm, 20 × 60 cm and 20 × 120 cm). The edges are tongue and groove. Laminated sections are laid on a level floor. Glue is applied to the grooves and then the sections are pressed together firmly. Laminated floor can be laid virtually anywhere in the home, even on top of old carpet or other floor-coverings.

VARIOUS DESIGNS

Laminated flooring is available in a very wide range of colors and designs, making it possible to combine different finishes together, such as a dark wood finish passageway in the hall with borders in a lighter wood finish that is then used in neighboring rooms. Alternatively, a patterned border may be used to mark off the seating area or another part of the floor covered with a different design. Maintaining laminated floors is an easy matter. The tough top layer is both dirt and water resistant. Vacuuming and an occasional going over with a mop are sufficient. A sponge floor mop with interchangeable heads is useful and can be quicker than a vacuum cleaner.

Spots such as grease, chocolate or wine can be removed with hot water and a gentle detergent. More stubborn stains such as shoe scuffs, cigarette marks, tar or soot should be cleaned with acetone or mineral spirits. Pencil can simply be rubbed out.

WOOD FLOORS

The various types of wood floors (boards, solid parquet or laminated parquet) have more or less the same properties. The base for these wooden floors has to be level, and wood can be laid on a solid floor.

Floating laminated wood floors, which are not fixed down but are laid directly on top of existing flooring, or on special felt, are becoming popular. If you select such a 'floating' floor, a lightly sprung layer is first rolled out across the floor and the wood is laid on top of this. This layer slightly deadens the sound and evens out any minor irregularities in the floor.

The parquet sections or boards are then fitted together with their tongues and grooves. Special edging strips keep the loose laid floor in place. A small expansion gap is left around the edge of the room between the wall and the wood floor, hidden under the baseboards or a strip of wood. This will prevent the floor from lifting in warm, humid conditions. There is another system with which the sections are held together with sprung metal clips. With this type it is possible to take the floor with you when you move.

For a fixed floor on a solid base, chipboard must first be laid to form a base. Be aware of any wiring or plumbing that exists under the floor. In many new homes, central heating coils and water pipes and electric conduits are run under concrete floors. Once this is fixed firmly in place, the wood floor can be nailed or glued to the

particleboard base.
If a wood floor is to be
laid on top of a plank
floor, it is straightforward.
Finally, it is possible to use
the existing timber boards
as flooring if it is in good
condition, or it can be
restored (see section on
repairing and restoring
wood floors, page 163).
Check the entire floor for
nails and screws from
previous floor coverings
before sanding. The floor
can be as good as new
after running over it with
a floor sander and treating
it with a floor finish. Bear
in mind that any
downstairs neighbours
will have problems with
noise if their ceiling is
right below your floor.

VARNISH OR WAX?

The finishing of a floor
can be done in a number
of ways. It can be painted
or stained to alter its color
and appearance, and
varnished, treated with oil
or waxed to protect it and
give it a shine. Which is
best depends upon the use
of the room and your
personal preference.
Polishing with wax needs
to be done more often
than varnishing, as does
the application of other
soft finishes, such as oil.
Some oil and wax polishes
are available with stains
mixed in to save having to
apply color separately.
Varnishes, too, are
available with color stains.
Varnish is best in several
coats and will give a
harder wearing finish;
however, it can be prone

to scratching or cracking,
especially from furniture,
and these marks are
harder to remove than
with wax. Gloss varnish
can also look less cozy
than wax.
With all types of stain or
wood dye, any remaining
paint or varnish needs to
be fully removed in order
to achieve an even finish,
and at least three coats of
stain or dye are required.
The alternatives are
almost endless. It is also
possible to buy finished
wood flooring that can be
walked on as soon as it is
laid.

MAINTENANCE

Maintenance of oiled or
waxed floors consists
mainly of vacuuming and
mopping. Special parquet
mops for use with a
vacuum cleaner can be
bought from companies
that supply parquet. The
layer of wax needs to be as
thin as possible because
thicker layers quickly
become dirty. Another
coat of wax is only needed
when the floor is nearly
bare of wax, and even then
only the worn areas
should be treated.
With a varnished floor the
daily cleaning consists
only of vacuuming. Stains
can usually be cleaned off
with a damp cloth. There
are various cleaning agents
available from builders
supply or flooring
companies for treating
more stubborn stains on
these floors.

The open fireplace

Open fires create a cozy atmosphere in the home. Regardless of whether the fireplace is a minimalist hole in a wall or a more grand affair built of sandstone with an antique mantle, it is the size of the chimney that determines how well the fire burns.

Almost every type of open fireplace can be built into a home, though in some circumstances the design of the chimney will have to be adapted.
Older houses usually have a fireplace, but often these are designed for coal- or gas-burning stoves. The diameter of the flue for these is much smaller than that needed for an open fire. Generally, an open fire needs a flue no smaller than 8 inches (20 cm). A fireplace installer or chimney sweep can assess your existing chimney. If there is no chimney it can be made using double-walled stainless steel tubing which is joined together with spring clips. The smooth inside of the flue ensures that the fire draws well. The system is available in various diameters. The right diameter depends upon the size of the fireplace. New ducted flues can often be fitted in existing chimneys. The flue needs to be as straight as possible and should have the same diameter throughout. The material has to cope with condensation, and insulation is important to prevent the flue from cooling too quickly.

UNUSUALLY SHAPED HEARTHS

For a hearth of unusual dimensions or with an unusually shaped opening, the fireplace needs to be built of firebricks, using fireproof mortar. With these materials, any kind of fireplace that is desired can be constructed. It is more usual, however, for people to select a standard hearth, with a hood of wrought iron or of special fire-resistant concrete. There is little difference in the quality.

ANDIRONS

It looks attractive to see the fire laid directly on a fireproof hearth, but if the fire will not burn very well, andirons might be the solution. Logs are placed on the andirons, which leaves room beneath for the ashes and embers. This makes it

> **START EARLY**
> The desire to create an open fireplace often happens in the autumn. Remember, however, that it can take months before a new fireplace can be lit for the first time because the construction has to harden. It is best dealt with by a specialist and started in the summer.

Grilling on charcoal between the kitchen and dining room.

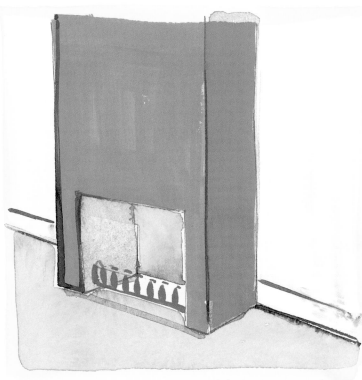

An attractive fireplace also adds style in the summer months.

easier to clean the fireplace. If you do not succeed with your first attempts to light a fire, there are specially made logs of pressed sawdust available that make it child's play.

VENTILATION WITH OPEN FIRES

Open fires use up lots of oxygen. This is drawn from the living area, making ventilation essential. It is possible, of course, to leave a window ajar, but this would largely negate the point of lighting the fire in the first place. More comfortable alternatives are to have special ventilation grills built into airbricks placed at baseboard height. These have the advantage

of not causing a draft while ensuring that the fire burns well.

ADJUSTING THE THERMOSTAT

By burning an open fire, the temperature in the room will rise and, if the main thermostat is located in the vicinity, the central

heating will switch itself off. The temperature elsewhere in the house will therefore become colder. You can avoid this by installing additional thermostats in other rooms so that temperature can be adjusted area-by area. If you use just the main thermostat, make sure it is as far away from the fireplace as possible, perhaps choosing the hall or dining-room as a more suitable location.

CARE WITH STOKING

To limit environmentally harmful waste products, it is best to stoke the fire with only dry, unpainted wood. Well-dried logs burn better, giving more heat, and less pollution

and soot in the chimney. Do not stoke the fire when it is foggy or there is no wind. The chimney will not draw correctly in this sort of weather and the fire will not burn properly. In addition, the smoke will probably hang in the air. Generally speaking, you can gauge that the lighter colored the smoke is, the cleaner the fire is burning.

OPTIMUM BURNING OPEN FIRE

A fire will not burn well with a chimney that does not draw properly. In such cases a flue ventilator that mechanically draws the flue gases upwards into the chimney is the solution. The equipment is placed in the chimney and is fully adjustable so that the precise draft can be created. They are available in models for both circular and rectangular section chimney flues, and for brick or metal flues. More information is available from a fireplace installer, a chimney sweep, or from manufacturers.

THE CHIMNEY: SWEEP AT LEAST ONCE A YEAR

Get a chimney sweep to clean the chimney before the start of the open fire season. A fire will burn properly only if the chimney is kept clean. The sweep can check the condition of the flue and trace any leaks.

ANTIQUE FIREPLACES

Old fireplaces are becoming increasingly popular and can be found at architectural salvage yards. Although in general the older the fireplace, the greater the value, fireplaces from some periods are less popular than others and the price will reflect this. Before installing an old fireplace, first make sure that it complies with today's safety regulations. Antique fireplaces are usually ideal for wood or other solid fuel fires, as this was what they were originally designed for, but some can also be adapted for flame effect fires using propane or natural gas. Another option is to buy a reproduction fireplace from the wide selection currently available.

The side of the chimney makes for fine shelf space.

The attic

The attic in many houses is frequently used for little more than storing unused items. Yet this space can quite easily be given a better use: perhaps as an extra bathroom, a work room or study, a separate floor for an au pair, or as a childrens' playroom. If an attic is to be used as a bedroom or living area it must be well ventilated and have sufficient daylight. Thorough insulation will be necessary to keep out the cold in winter and the heat in summer.

FIRST INSULATE

Before converting or re-arranging the attic, it is sensible to insulate it. See 'Insulation' on page 164 to find out how this can be done. Once the roof area has been insulated, you have a choice of how to finish the ceiling and walls. For a rustic or natural effect you can use tongue and groove boards. Finally, you can paint or stain the wood, to your personal taste.
If you decide upon sheetrock, the ceiling and walls can be plastered, painted or papered.

DORMER WINDOW

If the attic is somewhat small and dark, consider having a dormer built. Depending upon the existing space, this can provide a great deal more space (see illustration). Before making any alterations to the structure or appearance of your property, check that there are no restrictions or requirements imposed by the local authorities. Obtaining permission to make changes to buildings of historic importance or character may be difficult.

STANDARD OR MADE-TO-ORDER

Dormer extensions are available in prefabricated form from various manufacturers. For the design of a custom-made dormer, an architect, building surveyor or structural engineer are the appropriate professionals. They will draw the dormer that meets your needs and suits the style of your home. Once your chosen professional has prepared detailed plans, these can be used as the basis to obtain quotes from contractors. It may be convenient to ask your local contractor because they are likely to be aware of the local regulations. Always make sure that the contractor you hire has experience in handling similar work for other people. It is always sensible to ask for references and to check that previous clients were satisfied with their work.

WINDOWS

With one or more windows in the roof you can get plenty of natural light in the attic. Skylights are available in different types. The best known are the pivoting windows that are hinged in the middle. Where there is little headroom, a window hinged at the top may be preferable.
An unusual type is a balcony window, which consists of two windows on top of each other in the sloping roof. The upper window is hinged at the top while the lower window is hinged at the bottom.
The upper window opens to an almost horizontal position, the lower one to a vertical position. With a special fence on the side, it creates a 'balcony'.

EXTRA BATHROOM

An additional bathroom in the attic requires special considerations to deal with moisture. Particular attention needs to be given to ventilation and the location of the plumbing. Placement of the toilet and other fixtures must meet local codes, as well as be sensibly connected to the existing plumbing system. For information about ventilating bathrooms, see page 169. Another factor to bear in mind is the strength of the attic floor, and whether it will need additional support to cope with the extra weight.

A partition wall with shelving provides extra storage

Attic space without dormer window.

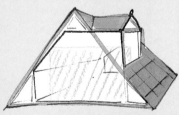

Extra headroom with dormer window.

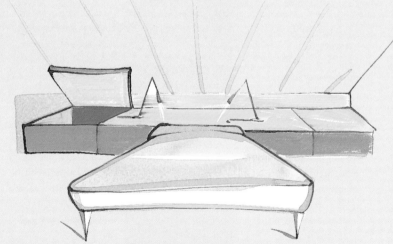

Where the ceiling is too low for seating, you can make extra storage space.

CONCEALING APPLIANCES

Some homes may have a hot water heater in the attic. This can usually be moved to a different, more convenient spot. Alternately, a partition wall or enclosure can be built to screen the tank. Such a partition has the added advantage of creating storage space, as shelves can be mounted on both sides of the wall.

CREATING STORAGE SPACE IN THE ATTIC

While the benefit of converting an attic is to provide extra sleeping or living space, the downside can be a loss of storage space. With good design, however, it is possible to maintain considerable storage space by building cabinets around the chimney or where the roof slope begins to meet the floor.

A high roof can provide the room for adding an additional floor between the ridge and the attic floor. This new loft can provide space to store things not in everyday use. This is a job for a professional because the roof must be able to bear the load of the new floor and storage.

COMPARE FIRST

Both architects and builders have their own terms and prices. Therefore you should ask for several estimates to compare before choosing. Confirm any agreements in writing, as far as possible, to prevent any problems later.

REPLACING TRUSSES

If your attic structure has lots of supports at eye level, it is possible to remove these so that you can stand upright, provided that additional support is created elsewhere. This is work for a professional or specialized contractor, because the loads on the roof and walls have to be calculated. If the floor of your attic has not been built to be used as a room, the beams will need to be strengthened, supported or replaced.

Security

Protecting your home against burglars is not just a matter of good locks. Deterring burglars in the first place is vital, so consider installing a burglar alarm or lights that come on when motion is detected. Good lighting in the garden and by entryways can also be a deterrent.

QUALITY LOCKS

Do not choose lower quality locks for doors that are out of sight. Back doors are more at risk of a break in than front doors. Old houses often have only doorknob locks. Such locks are easily opened. Replace these as a first priority with deadbolt locks.

SECURE EVEN THE SMALLEST VENT

The windows as well as the doors may need to be fitted with locks. Even the smallest window vent can be useful for the housebreaker. Surface locks, which are easy to fit yourself, are available for windows and shutters that open outwards. Locks for building into the frame are more suitable for windows that open both inwards and out. The

ONE KEY, MANY LOCKS

When there are a number of outside doors, including the garage, it is useful to have one key to fit all the outside doors. Have locks fitted that can all be opened with the same key, doing away with a bunch of keys.

Cylinder locks are more secure than simple lever locks.

window locks should also be capable of being opened with one key for safety reasons.

MORTISE BOLTS ARE ESSENTIAL

In addition to good locks, the hinges play a security role. Mortise bolts can be combined with the hinge. They connect the door and frame together so that the door is harder to force open and cannot be lifted off its hinges.

FITTING LOCKS: A CRAFT

It is best for locks to be fitted by a specialist, even for the good do-it-yourselfer. Some firms will give free advice on security matters and estimates. The type of locks that you have installed may qualify you for a discount on your homeowners insurance policy. Good locks may result in a real reduction in your premium.

EXTRA SECURE: A SAFE

A safe can be used for many things. Primarily, of course, it is useful for protecting valuables such as jewelery and cameras. But passports and insurance policies also deserve a safe place. Many safes also provide fire protection for important documents.

TYPES OF SAFES

There are furniture safes, wall safes and floor safes. A safe is of value only if it is firmly anchored to the structure of the house.

Security experts can advise you. They can also arrange to install the safe. Insurance companies sometimes insist that valuables are kept in a safe, although they may require the safe to be installed by the supplier.

LIGHTING AS DETERRENT TO BURGLARS

Lighting that scares off burglars is available in various types. One of the best known is a lighting fixture with a motion

Anti break-in strip for an inward opening door.

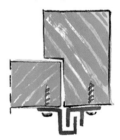

Anti break-in strip for an outward opening door.

The most secure method: the screws are hidden.

A hinge with a break-in resistant stud.

The pin ensures that the door cannot be forced off its hinges.

Window lock for surface fixing.

Window lock for mortise fitting.

detector which goes off if anyone moves within the beam from the sensor. These are particularly useful installed near the front door, because they are helpful to the homeowner hunting for keys at night and also illuminate a potential entry point for the would-be burglar. One sensor can control a number of lamps. These are available at hardware stores, builder supply stores, garden centers and lighting shops.

ALTERNATIVE: THE PHOTO-ELECTRIC CELL

Motion detectors have a disadvantage in that they can react to moving animals or, during stormy weather, to leaves and branches. If you find it a distraction to have the lights going on and off, there is an alternative. This is to control the lights with a photo-electric cell which will switch the lighting on at dusk and off at dawn.

INTERIOR LIGHTING

There are variations on this theme available for interior use too. Timer devices that plug into household sockets, and into which lamps are then plugged, can be set to go on and off so that the house looks occupied. You can purchase either a simple 24-hour timer or a more sophisticated seven-day version. Other similar devices turn on at dusk and off at dawn, while others still are noise-sensitive. So a knock or ring at the door will result in a light going on. Of course, not only lamps can be plugged into these timers: a radio or television could be used instead to give the impression that the house is occupied.

ALARMS

If all the other security systems are not sufficient, you can have an alarm system installed. Some set off flashing lights and sirens. The would-be burglar is usually long gone before the police are called. The alarm can be connected to a private security service. The people who work there can see from a code where the break in is happening and warn the police or their security company. Such systems can be silent or coupled to a lamp and siren. The installation of alarms and other security systems may reduce the cost of home insurance.

HOW DOES AN ALARM SYSTEM WORK?

Infrared movement detectors are installed at key places around the home and linked to each other and the alarm unit by wires. These detectors may be combined with pressure mats or switches that are triggered when certain doors or windows are opened. All of these items are linked together and any one of them may trigger the alarm.

Many alarms also have panic buttons located at strategic positions, such as by the front door and master bed.

By means of a code or a key, the system can be switched on or off at the control unit, although remote control units are also available. Some systems are designed to scare burglars or to warn the occupants or their neighbors of an intrusion. Maintenance and service costs have to be paid for systems that are connected to a central service.

Window catches with locks are also safer for children in high-rise apartments.

Mortise bolts can be fitted to frames, and screws can be replaced with mortise bolts on the other side of the window too. If the window opens, use an anti break-in strip.

Useful addresses

ANTIQUES

Architectural Antiques Exchange
715 N. Second St.
Philadelphia, PA 19123
(215) 922-3669

The Bank Architecturals
1824 Felicity St.
New Orleans, LA 70113
(504) 523-2702

The Brass Knob
2311 18th St., NW
Washington, D.C. 20009
(202) 332-3370

Coronado Wrecking and Salvage Co.
4200 Broadway, SE
Albuquerque, NM 87105
(505) 877-2821

Irreplaceable Artifacts
14 Second Ave.
New York, NY 10003
(212) 777-2900

Ohmega Salvage
2407 San Pablo Ave.
Berkeley, CA 94702
(510) 843-7368

The Renovation Source, Inc.
3512 N. Southport Ave.
Chicago, IL 60657
(773) 327-1250

BATHROOM

American Standard
PO Box 90318
Richmond, VA 23230
(800) 524-9797

Baths From the Past
83 E. Water St.
Rockland, MA 02370
(800) 697-3871

Bed, Bath, and Beyond
620 Avenue of the Americas
New York, NY 10011
(212) 255-3550

Delta Faucets
55 E. 11th St.
Indianapolis, IN 46280
(800) 345-3358

Sterling Plumbing Group, Inc.
2900 Golf Rd.
Rolling Meadows, IL 60007
(800) 783-7546

Urban Outfitters
4040 Locust St.
Philadelphia, PA 19104
(215) 569-3131

CABINETRY

KraftMaid Cabinetry, Inc.
16052 Industrial Parkway
Middlefield, OH 44087
(800) 770-6665

Siematic Corp.
One Neshaminy Interplex, Suite 207
Trevose, PA 19047
(800) 765-5266

UltraCraft
PO Box 1249
Liberty, NC 27298
(800) 262-4046

Wellborn Cabinet, Inc.
PO Box 1210
Ashland, AL 36251
(800) 336-8040

CATALOGUES

adaptAbility Catalog
PO Box 515
Colchester, CT 06415-0515
(800) 243-9232

Attitudes Catalog
1213 Elko Dr.
Sunnyvale, CA 94089
(800) 525-2468

Bristol Farms
606 Fair Oaks Ave.
S. Pasadena, CA 91030
(818) 441-5450

Chambers Catalog
PO Box 7841
San Francisco, CA 94120
(800) 334-9790

The Chefs Catalogue
3215 Commerical Ave.
Northbrook, IL 60662-1900
(800) 338-3232

Claiborne Gallery
608 Canyon Rd.
Santa Fe, NM 87501
(505) 982-8019

Colonial Garden Kitchen Catalog
PO Box 66
Hanover, PA 17333
(800) 258-6702

The Company Store
500 Company Store Rd.
La Crosse, WI 54601
(800) 442-2460

Coyote Café General Store
132 W. Water St.
Santa Fe, NM 87501
(800) 866-4695

Crate and Barrel Catalog
PO Box 3057
Northbrook, IL 60065
(800) 323-5461

Gardener's Eden Catalogue
PO Box 7307
San Francisco, CA 94120
(800) 822-9600

Gardener's Supply Co. Catalogue
128 Intervale Rd.
Burlington, VT 05401
(802) 863-1700

Hard-to-Find Tools Catalogue
1655 Bassford Dr.
Mexico, MO 65265
(800) 926-7000

Hold Everything
PO Box 7807
San Francisco, CA 94120
(800) 541-2233

Home Trends Catalog
1450 Lyell Ave.
Rochester, NY 14606
(716) 254-6520

IKEA
Plymouth Commons
Plymouth Meeting, PA 19462
(610) 834-0150

Pottery Barn
PO Box 7044
San Francisco, CA 94120
(800) 922-5507

Renovator's Supply Catalogue
PO Box 2515
Conway, NH 03818
(800) 659-0203

Solutions Catalogue
PO Box 6878
Portland, OR 97228
(800) 342-9988

Sundance Catalogue
780 W. 2400, South
Salt Lake City, UT 84120
(800) 422-2770

Williams Sonoma
PO Box 7456
San Francisco, CA 94120
(800) 541-2233

FABRICS, UPHOLSTREY, & WALL COVERINGS

Bradbury & Bradbury Wallpapers
940 Tyler St.
Benicia, CA 94510
(707) 746-1900

Calvin Klein Home
654 Madison Ave.
New York, NY 10022
(212) 292-9000

Delk & Morrison, Inc.
320 Julia St.
New Orleans, LA 70130
(504) 529-4939

George Smith
73 Spring St.
New York, NY 10012
(212) 226-4747

Kneedler-Faucher
8687 Melrose Ave.
Los Angeles, CA 90069
(310) 855-1313
or
101 Henry Adams St.
San Francisco, CA 94103
(415) 861-1011

Norton Blumenthal, Inc.
979 Third Ave.
New York, NY 10022
(212) 752-2535

Patina Finishes and Copper Coats
3486 Kurtz St. #102
San Diego, CA 92110
(800) 882-7004

Ralph Lauren Home Collection
980 Madison Ave.
New York, NY 10021
(212) 642-8700

Royal Design Studio
386 East H Street
Suite 209-188
Chula Vista, CA 91910
(800) 747-9767

FIREPLACES

Heat-n-Glo
6665 West Highway 13
Stowe, VT 05672
(800) 669-4328

FLOOR COVERINGS & CARPET

ABC Carpet & Home
888 Broadway
New York, NY 10003
(212) 674-1144

Azrock Industries
PO Box 3145
Houston, TX 77253
(800) 366-2689

Karastan Rugs
PO Box 12069
Calhoun, GA 30703
(800) 241-4494

Pergo
Perstorp Flooring, Inc.
524 New Hope Rd.
Raleigh, NC 27604
(800) 337-3746

FLOORS - STONE & TERRAZZO

Ann Sacks Tile & Stone, Inc.
8120 NE 33rd Dr.
Portland, OR 97211
(503) 284-1046

Bomanite Corp.
PO Box 599
Madera, CA 93639
(209) 673-2411

Cacallori Marble Co.
1535 S. Albro Place
Seattle, WA 98108
(206) 767-6300

Christie Cut Stone Co.
2029 Elzey Ave.
Memphis, TN 38104
(901) 274-0883

Midwest Marble Co.
510 S. Quincy Ave.
Tulsa, OK 74120
(918) 587-8193

Stone Products Corp.
PO Box 270
Napa, CA 94559
(800) 225-7462

Venetian Marble Co.
991 Harrison St.
San Francisco, CA 94107
(415) 392-6376

Westchester Marble & Granite, Inc.
610 S. Fulton Ave.
Mt. Vernon, NY 10550
(800) 634-0866

FLOORS - WOOD

Albany Woodworks
PO Box 729
Albany, LA 70711
(504) 567-1155

American Woodmark Corp.
3102 Shawnee Dr.
PO Box 1990
Winchester, VA 22601
(800) 388-2483

Armstrong World Industries
PO Box 3001
Lancaster, PA 17604
(800) 233-3823

Country Floors
15 East 16th St.
New York, NY 10003
(212) 627-8300

New England Hardwoods
Route 82 South
PO Box 534
Pine Plains, NY 12567
(518) 398-9663

FURNITURE

Aero
132 Spring St.
New York, NY 10012
(212) 966-1500

Arte de Mexico
1000 Chestnut St.
Burbank, CA 91506
(818) 508-0993

Barney's New York
106 Seventh Ave.
New York, NY 10011
(800) 929-9000

Fillamento
2185 Fillmore
San Francisco, CA 94115
(415) 931-2224

FreWil Furniture
605 North La Brea Ave.
Los Angeles, CA 90036
(213) 934-8474

Green Design Furniture
267 Commerical St.
Portland, ME 04101
(800) 853-4234

Limn
290 Townsend St.
San Francisco, CA 94107
(415) 543-5466

Mike Furniture
2142 Fillmore St.
San Francisco, CA 94115
(415)567-2700

Sauder Woodworking
502 Middle St.
Archbold, OH 43502
(800) 472-8337

Shabby Chic
1013 Montana Ave.
Santa Monica, CA 90403
(310) 394-1975
or
93 Greene St.
New York, NY 10012
(212) 274-9842

Slater Marinoff & Co.
1823 Fourth St
Berkeley, CA 94710
(510) 548-2001

Thomasville Furniture
PO Box 339
Thomasville, NC 27361
(800) 927-9202

Zona
97 Greene St
New York, NY 10012
(212) 925-6750

KITCHEN - APPLIANCES

AMANA
PO Box 8901
Amana, IL 52204
(800) 843-0304

Frigidare
(A Division of WCI
Major Appliance Group)
6000 Perimeter Dr.
Dublin, OH 43017
(800) 451-7007

**General Electric
GE Appliances**
Appliances Park
Louisville, KY 40225
(800) 626-2000

In-Sink-Erator
Emerson Electric Co.
4700 21st St.
Racine, WI 53406
(800) 558-5700

Sub-Zero Freezer Co.
PO Box 44130
4717 Hammersley Rd.
Madison, WI 53744
(800) 532-7820

Thermador
5119 District Blvd.
Los Angeles, CA
90040
(800) 656-9226

KITCHEN - COUNTERS & FLOORS

Corian Products
DuPont Co.
Wilmington, DE
19898
(800) 426-7426

Formica Corp.
10155 Reading Rd.
Cincinnati, OH
45241
(800) 367-5422

KITCHEN - GENERAL

Blanco
1001 Lower Landing
Rd., Suite 607
Blackwood, NJ 08012
(800) 451-5782

Bridge Kitchenware
214 E. 52nd St.
New York, NY 10022
(212) 688-4220

Franke
Kitchen Systems
Division
212 Church Rd.
North Wales, PA
19454
(800) 626-5771

**Heritage Custom
Kitchen**
215 Diller Ave
New Holland, PA
17557
(717) 354-4011

Homechef
3525 California St.
San Francisco, CA
94118
(415) 668-3191

Sur La Table
84 Pine St.
Seattle, WA 98101
(206) 448-2244

LIGHTING

Bulbtronics
PO Box 306
Farmingdale, NY
11735
(516) 249-2272

Fabby Lighting
450 S. La Brea Ave.
Los Angeles, CA
90036
(213) 939-1388

H.A. Framburg
941 Cernan Dr.
Bellwood, IL 60104
(800) 796-5514

**Lighting by Gregory,
Inc.**
158 Bowery
New York, NY 10012
(212) 226-1276

Lighting Unlimited
4025 Richmond Ave.
Houston, TX 77027
(713) 626-4025

Philips Lighting
200 Franklin Square Dr.
Somerset, NJ 08875
(800) 555-0050

SLD Lighting
318 West 47th St.
New York, NY 10036
(212) 245-4155

MOULDINGS & ORNAMENTATIONS

**American Custom
Millwork**
3904 Newton Rd.
PO Box 3608
Albany, GA 31706
(912) 888-3303

**Armstrong World
Industries Design
Resource Center**
PO Box 8022
Plymouth, MI 48170
(800) 704-8000

Coastcraft
1002 E. F St.
East Tacoma, WA
98401
(206) 272-1154

**Crown City
Hardware**
1047 N. Allen Ave.
Pasadena, CA 91104
(818) 794-1188

Decorator's Supply
3610-12 S. Morgan St.
Chicago, IL 60609
(773) 847-6300

Driwood Moulding Co.
623 W. Lucas St.
Florence, SC 29503
(803) 669-2478

**Restoration
Hardware**
6100 Topanga
Canyon Blvd.
Woodland Hills, CA
91367
(818) 887-7013

STAIRS

**Goodard
Manufacturing**
PO Box 502,
Dept. BH6-5
Logan, KS 67646
(913) 689-4341

Salter Industries
PO Box 183
Eagleville, PA 19408
(610) 631-1360

Stairways, Inc.
4166 Pinemont Dr.
Houston, TX 77018
(800) 231-0793

Unique Spiral Stairs
RRI Box 1220
Benton Rd.
Albion, ME 04910
(800) 924-2985

STOVES

Aga Cookers
17 Town Farm Lane
Stowe, VT 05672
(800) 633-9200

Best by Broan
926 West State St.
Hartford, WI 53027
(800) 692-7626

Jenn-Air
3035 N Shadeland
Indianapolis, IN
46226
(800) 688-1100

Russell Range, Inc.
229 Ryan Way
South San Francisco,
CA 94080
(415) 873-0105

Viking Range Corp.
111 W Front St.
Greenwood, MS
38930
(601) 455-1200

Wolf Range Co.
19600 S. Alameda St.
Compton, CA 90221
(310) 637-3737

TILE

**American Olean Tile
Company**
1000 N Cannon Ave
Lansdale, PA 19446
(215) 855-1111

Buddy Rhodes Studio
2130 Oakdale Ave.
San Francisco, CA
94124
(415) 641-8070

Dal-Tile
7834 Hawn Freeway
Dallas, TX 75217
(800) 933-8453

Hispanic Designe
6125 N. Cicero Ave.
Chicago, IL 60646
(773) 725-3100

**Reproduction
Ceramic Tile**
Richard Thomas
Keit Studios
206 Cañada St.
Ojai, CA 93023
(805) 640-9360

Seneca Tiles
7100 S. County Rd. #23
Attica, OH 44807
(419) 426-3561

**WINDOWS,
DOORS, BLINDS,
& SHUTTERS**

**American Blind &
Wallpaper Factory**
909 N. Sheldon Rd.
Plymouth, MI 48170
(800) 735-5300

Anderson Windows
100 Fourth Ave.
Bayport, MN 55003
(800) 426-4261

Baldwin Hardware
2675 Morgantown Rd.
Greenhills Corp.
Center, Suite 3200
Reading, PA 19607
(800) 566-1986

Hurd Windows
575 S. Whelen Ave.
Medford, WI 54451
(800) 223-4873

**National Blind &
Wallpaper Factory**
400 Galleria, Suite 400
Southfield, MI 48034
(800) 477-8000

**Pella Windows and
Doors**
102 Main St.
Pella, IA 50219
(800) 547-3552

**Pozzi Wood Windows
and Doors**
PO Box 5249
Bend, OR 97708
(800) 257-9663

**Timberlane
Woodcrafters**
903 B Easton Rd.
Warrington, PA 18976
(800) 250-2221

USA Blind Factory
1312 Live Oak St.
Houston, TX 77003
(800) 275-9426

**WROUGHT IRON
& METALWORKS**

Copperworks
400 Western Ave.
Petaluma, CA 94952
(707) 762-5530

**Harrington
Brass Works**
7 Pearl Ct
Allendale, NJ 07401
(201) 871-6011

Lux Metals
90 Ridgeway Ave.
Santa Rosa, CA
95406
(707) 546-1821

Strassen Plating
3619 Walton Ave
Cleveland, OH 44113
(216) 961-1525

MISC

**Ceramic Tile
Institute of America**
12061 Jefferson Blvd.
Culver City, CA
90230
(310) 574-7800

**Hardwood
Manufacturers
Association**
Department HI
400 Penn Center
Blvd., Suite 530
Pittsburgh, PA 15235
(800) 373-9663

**International
Association of
Lighting Designers**
18 East 16th St.
New York, NY 10003
(212) 206-1281

**Kitchen Cabinet
Manufacturers
Association**
1899 Preston White Dr.
Reston, VA 22091

**National Oak
Flooring
Manufacturers
Association**
22 North Front St.,
Suite 660
Memphis, TN 38103
(901) 526-5016

Index

ACKNOWLEDGMENTS

The author wishes to acknowledge the contribution made by the following at *VT Wonen*: Marita Janssen (editorial director); Iwona de Vos-Tuge (art director); Trudy Bruil (production designer); Rianne Landstra, Frans Bramlage, Marjan Godrie, Petra de Valk, Bastienne van Bockel (stylists); Tessa Jol, Dieuwke Marseille, Esther de Munnik (assistant stylists); Christine van der Hoff (chief sub-editor); Marc Hervermann, Laurens Keff, Karolien Knols (contributing editors); Saskia van der Maat, Jan Willem Papo (assistant editors).